CW00552325

Critical Guides to French Texts

109 Proust: A la recherche du temps perdu

Critical Guides to French Texts

EDITED BY ROGER LITTLE, WOLFGANG VAN EMDEN, DAVID WILLIAMS

PROUST

A la recherche du temps perdu

Richard Bales

Reader in French
Queen's University, Belfast

Grant & Cutler Ltd
1995

© Grant & Cutler Ltd 1995
ISBN 0 7293 0380 2

DEPÓSITO LEGAL: V. 4.794 - 1995

Printed in Spain by
Artes Gráficas Soler, S.A., Valencia
for
GRANT & CUTLER LTD
55-57 GREAT MARLBOROUGH STREET, LONDON W1V 2AY

Contents

Foreword

The aim of the present study is to provide some brief insights into a novel which is undoubtedly one of the greatest cultural artefacts of modern times. It cannot hope to cover every aspect of the exceptionally rich narrative which makes up *A la recherche du temps perdu*, nor does it attempt to address other facets of Proust's genius, such as his brilliance as a critic or as a letter-writer; a guide for further reading along these and other lines is offered in the bibliography. What I have tried to do, however, is to present a gradually unfolding account of some of the major features and themes of the novel, in an order which perhaps reflects a general reader's perception of priorities and difficulties. The summary which appears in the Appendix may, for all its brevity, help in fixing the overall shape of the novel in the reader's mind.

References to the text of *A la recherche du temps perdu* are to the Pléiade edition of 1987-89 (see *1* in the Select Bibliography). There are now so many paperback editions, with differing and ever-changing pagination, as to preclude reference to them as well. Quotations from other works are keyed to the bibliography by number and page, e.g., *47*, p.73.

I am exceptionally grateful to my friends Edward Hughes and Timothy Unwin for splendid advice they gave me as I was writing this book.

1. Genesis and Structure

Proust was always a prolific writer of texts, and there is much in his youthful productions which the latter-day reader can, with hindsight, point to as announcing future greatness: social analysis in some of the stories of *Les Plaisirs et les jours*, the heavily autobiographical bias of *Jean Santeuil*, aesthetic preoccupations in the works on Ruskin, to name just a few. But, as far as the genesis of *A la recherche du temps perdu* is concerned, the important date to remember is 1908, for, in a notebook attributable to that year (the *Carnet de 1908*), Proust jotted down a sort of progress report on an unnamed work he had embarked on. The precision of these jottings is such that one is presented with a virtually complete plan of *A la recherche du temps perdu*, including such famous scenes as the goodnight kiss, seaside encounters with young girls, and the uneven paving-stones which recall Venice; in addition, the theme of 'deux côtés' is evoked, as well as the imprisonment of a young girl; and finally, the notion of literary vocation is raised, concluding in a striking question from Proust to himself concerning the material he has at his disposal: 'Faut-il en faire un roman, une étude philosophique, suis-je romancier?' (*6*, p.61).

The question was not intended rhetorically, it was genuine. Proust was clearly in some doubt as to his literary vocation. For what he was engaged upon in the years 1908-09 was a curious hybrid work, 'le récit d'une matinée. Maman viendrait près de mon lit et je lui raconterais un article que je veux faire sur Sainte-Beuve' (*10*, VIII, p.320). Clearly, such an unpromising scenario was doomed to failure from the outset: one critic talking about another is bad enough, but communicating such criticism to a third party and, by extension, to potential readers would have been a hopeless proposition, and Proust eventually realised this. But the *Contre Sainte-Beuve* (as the manuscripts of this period which conform to

the announced 'récit' have come to be called) does address two
major preoccupations of *A la recherche du temps perdu* which make
much more sense when presented within the expanded format of a
novel proper: narration as a supremely personal act, necessitating
first-person presentation; and the articulation of literary theory, as
indispensable support and structure.

The *Contre Sainte-Beuve* is a sort of phantom text – one
which undeniably exists, but whose substance is elusive. The point
is that Proust was composing fragments which addressed important
topics, but the framework within which they were to be articulated
had not been decided upon: so, a given fragment will sometimes suit
an exclusively critical context, at other times a novelistic one, whilst
rarely satisfying both. This is the reason why it has been impossible
to publish a totally satisfactory, self-contained edition of the *Contre
Sainte-Beuve*. Most importantly, however, this 'récit' became re-
dundant by a sort of process of natural selection: Proust was fast
producing more and more material of a novelistic nature, edging out
the narrowly critical sections. With seamless fluidity, from the
springtime of 1909 onwards, the manuscripts 'prennent l'allure, le
ton, les proportions d'un véritable roman' (I, p.lvi).

At this point, it will be as well to say a word or two about
Proust's manuscripts as a whole: the insights they provide into his
working methods are not only interesting in themselves, they also
provide valuable clues to the manner in which *A la recherche du
temps perdu*, as total novelistic enterprise, developed.

Typically, Proust would take a school exercise book and
produce a rough first draft of an episode, perhaps just a few lines
long, perhaps a couple of pages. Further on in the same exercise
book, other episodes would appear, equally brief, but, within their
brevity, complete – they are not telegrammatic jottings. Then,
perhaps in the same book, and certainly in other books – sometimes
very many of them – these passages will be reworked, endlessly
crossed out and emended, lengthened or shortened, generally
polished. Only after separate work on individual episodes does
Proust proceed to copying out a more or less continuous text which
accumulates several episodes – 'more or less continuous' because

points of transition between episodes are often jerky at this point. The next stage in the process is to have this latest version typed by a secretary, the resultant typescript being considered by Proust as fair game for a further round of reworking in great detail. That in turn is more often than not followed by a fresh typescript, incorporating the manuscript changes, and so the process continues. Even when proof stage is reached, Proust is still correcting with a vengeance, the despair of his printers.

It is not just that Proust was a perfectionist – on the contrary, he could often be slapdash. What is important to pinpoint in this working process is that the basic elements from which he worked – individual fragments, isolated episodes – act as so many cells which take on a life of their own, and organically expand and interact, as if they constitute a living, growing body. There appears to be a limit-less elasticity, an unbounded dynamism to this seemingly haphazard method, to such an extent that study of Proust's manuscripts, far from being a dry exercise in literary archaeology, affords on the contrary an exciting glimpse into the first stirrings of genius. Publication of the preliminary *esquisses*, notably in the latest Pléiade edition of *A la recherche du temps perdu*, is now making much of this material available to non-specialists.

The elasticity of which I have just spoken proved to be invaluable as Proust's work stretched over the years: it permitted him to incorporate into a pre-existent structure new elements which could not have been foreseen at the time of planning – the 1914-1918 war, for example. What, however, cannot be explained by recourse to the manuscripts, is the unerring manner in which Proust constructs a glorious narrative sweep from episodes assembled apparently pell-mell, and is able to maintain huge constructional arches over thousands of pages: however particular any given episode in hand may be, its place in the general framework is always crystal-clear. This overall planning on the grand scale seems, astonishingly, to have existed in Proust's mind, and there alone.

Of course, written skeletons existed too, including the one in the *Carnet de 1908* alluded to above, and eventually, fleshed out, they became the volumes which we know as *A la recherche du temps perdu*. But the story of their production is predictably complicated. For a start, the overall title of the novel was different: right up to 1913 it was *Les Intermittences du cœur*, a good enough title in itself, so much so that Proust saved it for a sub-section of *Sodome et Gomorrhe*. Two parts to the novel were envisaged: *Le Temps perdu* and *Le Temps retrouvé*, and much of this relatively short version was written by about 1911. But the elasticity of Proust's method was already at work here, and his natural bent for expansion necessitated a third, intermediary, volume called *Le Côté de Guermantes*, at which point the first volume was renamed *Du côté de chez Swann*, thus producing a new symmetry of titles.

A further complication was that when Proust eventually found a publisher willing to take on such a hopelessly chaotic author (after several rejections, he found one (Grasset), but had to pay all his own printing costs), the first volume (1913) had to be cut off at an arbitrary point, simply because the book could not contain any more pages, and the residue became part of the then second volume, *Le Côté de Guermantes*. The knock-on effect of this displacement was now to be exacerbated by an apparently extraneous event: the outbreak of war in 1914. In that year, the second volume was being set up, and Proust was engaged in correcting the proofs, when the cessation of all inessential work put paid to the possibility of any publication for the duration of hostilities. This is the point at which the elasticity factor came into operation most fully: with the printing presses stopped, Proust vastly expanded his original plan, notably reworking the first part of the intended second volume, to produce a brand-new volume entitled *A l'ombre des jeunes filles en fleurs*, intercalated between *Du côté de chez Swann* and an extended *Côté de Guermantes*. The development of Albertine as a major character dates from this period.

Once the war was over, composition continued in a more orderly fashion, with publication of volumes following a fairly rapid rhythm. After the shaky pre-war reception to *Du côté de chez Swann*, Proust suddenly became famous in 1919, with the attribution of the Prix Goncourt, and the celebrated *Nouvelle Revue Française* enthusiastically took over publication. Although he died before the final volumes could appear, and there are many roughnesses, inconsistencies and lacunae in these later sections, *A la recherche du temps perdu* is a finished novel in the sense that its conclusion is resoundingly one of consummation. It can only be considered unfinished by those who demand the last degree of polish from an author who always laid greater stress on fertility of invention than on orderliness of presentation.[1]

As we have seen, *A la recherche du temps perdu* was subject to a quite unusual degree of recasting and alteration over the years. Nevertheless, at any given moment of its elaboration, the overall structure was clearly in view, and is ceaselessly underlined by Proust, whether in his correspondence or in print, and it is this insistence on structure which permits – and controls – intermediary enlargement. However massive this expansion, the plan could always accommodate it without the narrative thread being broken. Why should this be so?

The basic answer is a simple one, already announced in the novel's title: the plot of *A la recherche du temps perdu* is essentially that of a *quest*, that is, travel towards a goal which can lie further away or nearer, and whose attainment, though probable, is by its very nature unpredictable. Such travel could of course all too easily become mere drift, hence Proust's care to underline structural features, which must give shape to what is seemingly random. For if *A la recherche du temps perdu* contains inscribed within itself a programme of closure and achievement, it also allows in the process areas of openness, incompletion, scenarios of the unforeseen and the unforeseeable, unrealised possibilities. It is in the dialectic of these ostensibly antagonistic categories that much of Proust's strength as

---

[1] In the last few years, it has become apparent (from discoveries in the manuscripts) that towards the end of his life Proust envisaged considerable reorganisation of the final stages of his novel, work which he failed to complete before his death. It would have involved enormous excisions in what we now know as *Albertine disparue*, followed by consequential alterations. For an excellent summary of this complex issue, see Jean Milly, 'Faut-il changer la fin du roman de Proust?', *Etudes françaises* (Presses de l'Université de Montréal), été 1994, pp.15-40.

a writer resides.

In some ways, *A la recherche du temps perdu* is best viewed as a sort of 'Bildungsroman', that German genre in which the hero's development from childhood is traced through many vicissitudes to enlightened maturity. Or it could be seen as a latter-day *Pilgrim's Progress* – but a secular one, where the hero has to undergo various social and artistic trials before achieving a hard-won mastery. An even more ambitious parallel would be with another very religious work, Dante's *Divine Comedy*, where there is an analogous tracing of an individual's development which leans heavily on literary expression bordering on the spiritual.

Whether or not these comparisons are valid, one thing is sure: works of this kind, which could conceivably be expanded or contracted at will, require firm structures and clear patterning devices to underpin what risks becoming directionless activity. Dante is particularly famous for this; but it is no less true of Proust. Already, *Du côté de chez Swann* in one of its roles – that of composite introductory volume – sets out geographical and social parameters to which the rest of the novel will never cease to refer: the childhood paradise of Combray, where the Narrator associates middle-class values with one particular country walk (le côté de chez Swann), and aristocratic ones with another (le côté de Guermantes), and never the twain shall meet, either from a topographical or from a social point of view. When the Narrator is eventually proven wrong on both scores (on the geography, as late as *Le Temps retrouvé*), we witness the point of closure of a theme which has been sustained over the full length of the novel: yes, the middle classes represented by Swann and the aristocracy represented by the Guermantes are indeed compatible, merging together in the shape of Mlle de Saint-Loup, fruit of the marriage between the Guermantes Robert de Saint-Loup and Gilberte Swann. What seemed impossible is in the end quite simply achieved, just as the path which led past Swann's did after all join up with the one past the Guermantes'.

Geographical structuring is also particularly apparent in that part of *A l'ombre des jeunes filles en fleurs* which takes place at the seaside resort of Balbec. Staying as he does at the Grand-Hôtel, which is right by the sea, the Narrator is the constant witness to the interplay of interiors and exteriors, the sea and the land, being enclosed and being out in the open. Encountering new people in these situations, dining with them, going on excursions with them, by carriage or by local narrow-gauge railway – these all become so many little structural cells capable of infinite development and expansion. Indeed, the whole Balbec section of *A l'ombre des jeunes filles en fleurs* is itself recapitulated in an equivalent section of *Sodome et Gomorrhe*, and variations are performed on the social and geographical mini-structures introduced on that first occasion. And even before Balbec has been visited, the Narrator, in fantasising about the wildness of the place, turns it into a potentially major thematic entity – which of course it becomes.

But the place which figures more than any other, with massive structural importance, is Paris. All other places are defined by reference to it; it is truly the centre of existence of the novel. As in Balzac, it is the theatre of so many superficial triumphs, so many wrecked ambitions, not least in the career of the Narrator himself, for it is resolutely in a Parisian context that his social and literary apprenticeships are acted out. On a social level, the reception scenes – some of them several hundred pages long – form great structural pillars supporting much of the middle part of the novel, while on the intimate level of the Narrator's affair with Albertine a much greater fluidity of structure is visible (it can sometimes seem an absence of structure), for the reason that she provides the sole guiding thread – in her presence and in her absence – for vast areas of the novel.

All paths lead inexorably back to Paris. For if there is un-questionably an important patterning feature in travelling away from Paris, travelling back to it is possibly an even more striking configuration. There are numerous such journeys in *A la recherche du temps perdu*, but towards the end of the novel their rhythm accelerates noticeably. First, the trip back from an impromptu visit to Venice, where the Narrator has had his faith in art greatly restored, will be the prelude to enormous social changes – the letter he reads on the journey announcing the forthcoming marriage of

Saint-Loup and Gilberte Swann is but a foretaste of what is to come, culminating in the war, which will transform everything. During all this time, the Narrator, having clearly had a nervous breakdown, makes stays in various sanatoria from which he returns to the capital on three occasions (IV, pp.301, 315, 433). This bunching of return journeys takes on a persistence which reflects the Narrator's increasing realisation that now or never is the time for him to fulfil his literary vocation. As he sits in the train, viewing through the window, unmoved, a scene of natural beauty, his immediate verdict is negative: 'Si j'ai jamais pu me croire poète, je sais maintenant que je ne le suis pas' (IV, p.433). But this negative assessment will ironically turn out in a positive light, when the episode of which it forms a part is transfigured in the sequence of three 'moments bienheureux' which will finally spur him on to achieving his goal. And this threefold sequence, like the barren return trips to Paris, represents a clearly contoured pattern, though this time fruitful.

These patterns of repetition, whilst not obtrusive, are nevertheless insistent: necessarily so, for time is running out for the Narrator, and if he is to produce his work of art, he must set to work without delay. So, when he does take the plunge, he automatically incorporates into his preliminary thoughts the sort of patterning procedures just evoked. In effect, his experiences of 'moments bienheureux' in *Le Temps retrouvé* allow him to look back and perceive structure in a past life which seemed formless at the time; and, moreover, as he puts it, 'je compris que tous ces matériaux de l'œuvre littéraire, c'était ma vie passée' (IV, p.478). 'Matériaux' is a key word here – it presupposes self-conscious structuring; and, sure enough, what the Narrator does at about this point is engage upon a series of theoretical meditations on the nature of literature, in so many rapid 'bites' whose rhythm recalls that of the Paris-bound journeys or the 'moments bienheureux' of *Le Temps retrouvé*; here, theory drawn out of experience becomes the basis for the work to be. Thus the ending of the Narrator's career as protagonist and the beginning of his new career as novelist overlap and they do so appropriately enough in the intermeshing of formal features, thereby strengthening the indivisibility of the two

narratorial functions and underlining the rhetorical statement that
'la vraie vie, la vie enfin découverte et éclaircie, la seule vie par
conséquent pleinement vécue, c'est la littérature' (IV, p.474). And,
at a further remove, the reader can recognise that these principles
which the Narrator proposes to adopt in his forthcoming venture
have been the selfsame ones which have underpinned the novel we
have just read, that is Proust's. Such pleasing symmetries are
eloquent in their very simplicity.

2. The Narrator

Who is this Narrator whose life constitutes the subject-matter of the vast enterprise entitled *A la recherche du temps perdu*? He is a singularly shadowy figure, much less substantial in many ways than most of the characters who surround him, and this in spite of the fact that he is a constant presence as far as the reader is concerned. There is a certain irony here: first-person narration, far from providing ready access into the narrating individual's mind, constitutes a form of occlusion, as much as to say that it is more difficult for a person to talk about himself than about others. The very anonymity of the Narrator of *A la recherche du temps perdu* speaks volumes on this score. (The name 'Marcel' does, it is true, occur a couple of times late on in the novel as a name by which Albertine *might have* called the Narrator, if the latter had possessed the same name as the *author*, but this is in a part of the novel which Proust did not live to correct: it is an anomaly which is probably best ignored for the sake of consistency – for nearly 100 per cent of the novel, the Narrator is anonymous.)

Certainly, lack of a name is wholly consistent with the virtual lack of being with which the emergent personality of the Narrator is endowed in the first few pages of the novel. In these chaotic sequences which present overlapping areas of temporal and spatial existence in the borderline zone of sleeping and waking, he possesses 'seulement dans sa simplicité première, le sentiment de l'existence comme il peut frémir au fond d'un animal'; he is 'plus dénué que l'homme des cavernes' (I, p.5), his awareness 'hésitait au seuil des temps et des formes' whilst everything 'tournait autour de [lui] dans l'obscurité, les choses, les pays, les années' (I, p.6). Insecurity permeates every feature of these opening pages, and it is only with difficulty that some sort of order is pieced together out of wholesale confusion.

It is the beginning of the Narrator's voyage of self-discovery, embarked upon by way of disjointed forays into his own past, in order to try and perceive some sort of inherent pattern. This of course proves impossible, and all he can salvage, in this section of *Combray*, is a few anecdotes, albeit vivid ones – the magic lantern, Swann's visits, his mother's goodnight kiss. A rational and self-conscious attempt to recall the past – voluntary memory – is a fruitless exercise. Only an unexpected unleashing of concealed mental reserves – involuntary memory – provides a coherence which comes with total recall. These overwhelming occasions, often termed 'moments bienheureux', punctuate the Narrator's life at irregular intervals, and provide his existence with a metaphysical dimension which contrasts with his day-to-day being. Indeed, this sort of duality is a constant feature of his life: at one moment he leads a humdrum existence, at the next he is a visionary. And, importantly, this duality is itself situated within another framework of inbuilt duality.

For it is crucial to remember that the Narrator, in seeking to recapture the past, is thereby necessarily acknowledging the existence of a gulf lying between it and the present in which he is working, and that the person doing the investigating is in many ways different from the one being investigated, even though they are technically 'the same'. In other words, the passage of time creates difference, a difference which it is the Narrator's quest to abolish. Thus, at any given moment one is faced not just with the one Narrator, but with a multiplicity of them, for he evolves even as he writes. To take the simplest case, the experiences of childhood narrated in *Combray* must necessarily be relayed through the intermediary of an older person, who is of course the youngster grown up, and therefore subject to the difference just mentioned. But the relationship of older to younger Narrator is itself a fluid one, for each is in its own state of separate development, neither of them being fixed for any appreciable period of time. And the fact that the Narrator, at whatever stage of his career he may be, must necessarily always use the pronoun 'je', far from simplifying matters, only serves to confuse them further by eliding difference where we know it must exist. A reading of *A la recherche du temps perdu* rapidly makes one aware of the protean nature of the Narrator, presenting as he does many different aspects, both to himself and to the reader. He encapsulates the very notion of human change.

As far as the two sides to the Narrator's personality are concerned – the mundane and the visionary – the first is readily accessible as the story unfolds. The second, however, requires some illustration. It is quite clear that the youthful Narrator, from an early stage in his development, is sensitive to areas of perception lying beyond everyday reality: the experiences are rare, it is true, but their paucity is more than adequately recompensed by their power. On country walks, for example, the woods around 'entendaient des cris joyeux, qui n'étaient [...] que des idées confuses qui m'exaltaient et qui n'ont pas atteint le repos dans la lumière, pour avoir préféré, à un lent et difficile éclaircissement, le plaisir d'une dérivation plus aisée vers une issue immédiate' (I, p.153). On one of these occasions, the discrepancy between the feeling experienced and the manner of expressing it is soberly put:

> Le toit de tuile faisait dans la mare, que le soleil rendait
> de nouveau réfléchissante, une marbrure rose, à laquelle
> je n'avais encore jamais fait attention. En voyant sur
> l'eau et à la face du mur un pâle sourire répondre au
> sourire du ciel, je m'écriai dans mon enthousiasme en
> brandissant mon parapluie refermé: 'Zut, zut, zut, zut.'
> Mais en même temps je sentis que mon devoir eût été de
> ne pas m'en tenir à ces mots opaques et de tâcher de
> voir plus clair dans mon ravissement. (I, p.153)

This extreme sensitivity – not just the 'ravissement' itself, but more importantly the recognition that analysis of it, foregone in this instance, is an essential component to the complete sensation – is clearly that of a precocious child (he would be about seven or eight at the time); but it is also perfectly clear from the older Narrator's careful, if censuring, presentation of his younger self's experiences

that much of what is to come in his life has its beginnings here.
Time and again, we are told of how the child apprehended an
unseen dimension to things: Combray church, with its fourth
dimension of time (I, p.60); a row of hawthorn bushes (I, p.136);
church spires viewed from a distance (I. p.178). Typically, the new
perspectives opened up are experienced in brimming moments, yet
the fullness of their secret is never explained, and a feeling of
dissatisfaction results. Exceptionally, however, the Narrator does
make the extra effort involved in the case of the church spires, and
drives beyond the immediate euphoria:

> Je ne savais pas la raison du plaisir que j'avais eu à les
> apercevoir à l'horizon et l'obligation de chercher à
> découvrir cette raison me semblait bien pénible; j'avais
> envie de garder en réserve dans ma tête ces lignes
> remuantes au soleil et de n'y plus penser maintenant. Et
> il est probable que si je l'avais fait, les deux clochers
> seraient allés à jamais rejoindre tant d'arbres, de toits,
> de parfums, de sons, que j'avais distingués des autres à
> cause de ce plaisir obscur qu'ils m'avaient procuré et
> que je n'ai jamais approfondi. (I, p.178)

'Approfondir' is a key word, and it will crop up time and time
again; on this occasion, the Narrator does indeed go beyond the
experience, and 'fixes' it by writing a kind of prose-poem which,
however, remains purely on the descriptive level and attempts no
analysis. He had been 'débarrassé de ces clochers et de ce qu'ils
cachaient derrière eux'; he is like a hen who has laid an egg and
celebrates by proceeding to 'chanter à tue-tête' (I, p.180). But the
whole matter is infinitely more serious than this: on either side of
the evocation of Combray by involuntary memory, the older
Narrator makes sonorous reference to a deeper part of his self. In
summing up what Combray means to him, 'c'est surtout comme à
des gisements profonds de mon sol mental, comme aux terrains
résistants sur lesquels je m'appuie encore, que je dois penser au côté
de Méséglise et au côté de Guermantes' (I, p.182). And perhaps

even more graphically, in the build-up to the madeleine episode, 'je sens tressaillir en moi quelque chose qui se déplace, voudrait s'élever, quelque chose qu'on aurait désancré, à une grande profondeur; je ne sais ce que c'est, mais cela monte lentement; j'éprouve la résistance et j'entends la rumeur des distances traversées' (I, p.45). These are weighty matters indeed, and the Narrator is acutely aware that they should not be irreverently brushed aside.

So it is also that the Narrator lays very great stress on one aspect of human existence constantly experienced, yet underrepresented in literature – the world of dreams. Few writers can have investigated this area as fully as Proust. The whole of the opening sequence of *Du côté de chez Swann* pays explicit tribute to the massive place which dreams hold in one's life – 'Un homme qui dort, tient en cercle autour de lui le fil des heures, l'ordre des années et des mondes' (I, p.5) – and Proust never lets slip an opportunity of displaying just how predominant they are in the life of the Narrator. The general effect of this stress is to endow the unconscious life with a validity which almost, if not indeed totally, equates it with the world of wakefulness, so much so that on one occasion, when reflecting on a 'morceau de paysage' which floats to the top of his memory, the Narrator wonders 'de quel pays, de quel temps – peut-être tout simplement de quel rêve – il vient' (I, p.182).

Daydreams too play a considerable role in the Narrator's make-up, particularly in his younger days. Thus, walking past the Guermantes park, ludicrously, 'Je rêvais que Mme de Guermantes m'y faisait venir, éprise pour moi d'un soudain caprice; tout le jour elle y pêchait la truite avec moi' (I, p.170). Such fantasies abound in the boy's vivid imagination, and nicely point up the tongue-in-cheek consideration of his earlier self by the mature Narrator. But in another area, these daydreams are deadly serious, and he views them as his true *raison d'être*. The sentence just quoted has the following sequel:

Elle [Mme de Guermantes] me faisait lui dire le sujet
des poèmes que j'avais l'intention de composer. Et ces

rêves m'avertissaient que puisque je voulais un jour être un écrivain, il était temps de savoir ce que je comptais écrire. Mais dès que je me le demandais, tâchant de trouver un sujet où je pusse faire tenir une signification philosophique infinie, mon esprit s'arrêtait de fonctionner, je ne voyais plus que le vide en face de mon attention, je sentais que je n'avais pas de génie ou peut-être une maladie cérébrale l'empêchait de naître.

(I, p.170)

The whole of the Narrator's life-story is here in germ. The fantasies, by dint of self-indulgent exaggeration, become unrealisable; the end is visualised without the means being considered; sights are set impossibly high ('une signification philosophique infinie'); and inevitably dejection and lack of self-confidence result.

This depressive syndrome naggingly tracks the Narrator throughout his career, and deals him heavy blows just when he would wish to be uplifted and succeed in doing justice to his metaphysical experiences. So when, in *A l'ombre des jeunes filles en fleurs*, he is out riding in a carriage with Mme de Villeparisis near Balbec, the sight of three trees fills him with a 'bonheur profond' (II, p.76), analogous to that produced by the Martinville steeples; but the experience remains incomplete, and he fails to uncover what lies beneath the vision, that which would lead him to 'commencer enfin une vraie vie' (II, p.77). The last words of the episode are infinitely melancholy: 'j'étais triste comme si je venais de perdre un ami, de mourir à moi-même, de renier un mort ou de méconnaître un dieu' (II, p.79). Then again, in *Le Temps retrouvé*, a similar experience of looking at trees – but a cold, unemotional one this time – leads the Narrator to exclaim to himself: 'Arbres [...], vous n'avez plus rien à me dire, mon cœur refroidi ne vous entend plus. [...] Si j'ai jamais pu me croire poète, je sais maintenant que je ne le suis pas' (IV, p.433). Here, the Narrator is at his lowest ebb (indeed, he is on his way back from unsuccessful treatment in a 'maison de santé'), and the line seems finally to be drawn under his pretensions to being an artist. Yet this is to reckon without the tenacity of his obsession with art.

For the Narrator's is a true vocation to art – it is the be-all and end-all of his existence. In the narration of childhood represented by *Combray*, we constantly obtain glimpses of the young boy reading in the garden, or lying on his bed. His thirst for reading-matter is insatiable, and his expectations high: 'ce qu'il y avait d'abord en moi, de plus intime, [...] c'était ma croyance en la richesse philosophique, en la beauté du livre que je lisais, et mon désir de me les approprier, quel que fût ce livre' (I, p.83). His role model, the fictional novelist Bergotte, quite bowls him over ('il exprimait toute une philosophie nouvelle pour moi par de merveilleuses images', I, p.93), and will go on to become one of the three artistic guiding spirits of his adulthood. Note that word 'philosophie' again: employed liberally in a general sense to designate realms of lofty idealism, it simultaneously acts as a magnet for the Narrator's aspirations and, as we have seen earlier on, points up the realisation that his own feeble mind, and the works of art he aims to produce, can never hope to match up to such heights.

Yet, in parallel with the sublimity which Bergotte exemplifies, there exists an altogether more modest reading experience, and one which will surprisingly turn out to be more durable – indeed, it will be crucial for the fulfilment of the Narrator's vocation. It is the small collection of George Sand novels which his grandmother gives him for his birthday. As we are told, 'elle ne se résignait jamais à rien acheter dont on ne pût tirer un profit intellectuel' (I, p.39), and her grandson is the willing recipient of her cultural largesse – they are clearly kindred spirits, and will remain so until her death, which is so traumatic for him. *François le Champi* in particular, because of 'sa couverture rougeâtre et son titre incompréhensible' provides him with 'une personnalité distincte et un attrait mystérieux', so that 'sous ces événements si journaliers, ces choses si communes, ces mots si courants, je sentais comme une intonation, une accentuation étrange' (I, p.41).

George Sand's name scarcely ever reappears after this child-hood idyll spent reading her novels; that is, not until the scene in *Le Temps retrouvé* where the Narrator is left alone in the Guermantes' library. Flicking idly through the books, he comes upon a copy of the same edition of *François le Champi* as he had read as a child, and instantly feels he is in the presence of a stranger. Who could it be? Suddenly he realises:

> Cet étranger, c'était moi-même, c'était l'enfant que
> j'étais alors, que le livre venait de susciter en moi, car
> de moi ne connaissant que cet enfant, c'est cet enfant
> que le livre avait appelé tout de suite, ne voulant être
> regardé que par ses yeux, aimé que par son cœur, et ne
> parler qu'à lui. (IV, p.463)

The affection is clearly deep-seated, and has been preserved over the years, albeit unacknowledged until now; and it is all the more vivid and authentic for that very absence. The superficialities of the years are swept aside: 'c'est à une [grande] profondeur [...] que j'avais plongé' (IV, p.462).

This desire to reach down into the depths of experience seems to be a constant and insatiable need for the Narrator, a distinguishing psychological trait. On one occasion, he is lost in wonder before a row of hawthorn bushes near Combray, but repeated observation and meditation fail to push the experience any further:

> Elles [les aubépines] m'offraient indéfiniment le même
> charme avec une profusion inépuisable, mais sans me
> laisser approfondir davantage, comme ces mélodies
> qu'on rejoue cent fois de suite sans descendre plus avant
> dans leur secret. (I, p.136)

This is clearly the younger Narrator's experience, even if it requires the adult language of the older Narrator to give shape to what must have been inchoate feelings rather than a verbally articulated concept. It is a case amongst many of the older Narrator's extrapolating from his earlier experience, and drawing a theory of profundity out of it.

The process can be seen at its clearest in the coda to *Combray*, where the older Narrator provides, simultaneously, a reflective view of what Combray meant to him, and a general meditation on some of his own character-traits. The connection between his past in Combray and the present in which he is writing could scarcely be closer when he declares that thinking of the Méséglise and Guermantes ways reveals 'des gisements profonds de [son] sol mental' (I, p.182). It is to these geographical localities in their psychological extension that he never ceases to refer: from them, his 'impressions d'aujourd'hui' receive 'de la profondeur, une dimension de plus' (I, p.183). It is above all a question of emotional ties, where the simplest of objects create the greatest ardour: 'les bleuets, les aubépines, les pommiers qu'il m'arrive quand je voyage de rencontrer encore dans les champs, parce qu'ils sont situés à la même profondeur, au niveau de mon passé, sont immédiatement en communication avec mon cœur' (I, p.182).

Finally, it comes as no surprise that in the concluding peroration of the whole novel the theme of depth and its indissociability with the Narrator's priorities in life receives its definitive treatment. Death, which hovers so threateningly – yet creatively – over these pages, takes up residence in the Narrator's mind, and 'sa pensée adhérait à la plus profonde couche de mon cerveau' (IV, p.619). The proximity of death, both to himself and to those he sees around him, causes him to reflect on the past with ever greater poignancy, as here in recalling the garden-gate bell, one of his earliest memories:

> Pour tâcher de l'entendre [la sonnette] de plus près, c'est en moi-même que j'étais obligé de redescendre. C'est donc que ce tintement y était toujours, et aussi, entre lui et l'instant présent tout ce passé indéfiniment déroulé que je ne savais pas que je portais. Quand elle avait tinté, j'existais déjà, et depuis pour que j'entendisse encore ce tintement, il fallait qu'il n'y eût pas eu discontinuité, que je n'eusse pas un instant cessé, pris le repos de ne pas exister, de ne pas penser, de ne

> pas avoir conscience de moi, puisque cet instant ancien
> tenait encore à moi, que je pouvais encore le retrouver,
> retourner jusqu'à lui, rien qu'en descendant plus
> profondément en moi. (IV, pp.623-24)

So it is that in bridging the gap which seemed invariably to exist
between the present-day Narrator and his younger self – the gulf of
time which appeared so destructive – another rift is breached: by
recognising that the notion of depth can possess a dimension other
than the spatial, downward one, he manages to perceive the means
by which the past can be salvaged in its entirety. By probing more
deeply into himself, sideways, as it were, he permits the past to be
'indéfiniment déroulé', as a seamless whole. It is a staggering
feeling – 'J'avais le vertige de voir au-dessous de moi, *en moi
pourtant*, comme si j'avais des lieues de hauteur, tant d'années' (IV,
p.624; my emphasis) – but at last the Narrator is a unified
personality with a clear insight into the pattern of his existence. He
is now fully equipped to embark on the production of the work of art
which he long felt was within him.

3. Places and People

Being capacious, *A la recherche du temps perdu* not surprisingly contains a great wealth of characters. All human life is here: actresses, waiters, duchesses, chauffeurs, lift-attendants, soldiers, musicians. The variety is endless. But the cast-list is eminently manageable for the reader, because the really important characters are relatively few in number. Besides, they are intimately tied to the geographical locations within which they are first encountered, and they assume a physical solidity which instantaneously makes them memorable. Most important of all, it is the Narrator's travels which occasion the encounters: we meet new people exactly when and where he comes upon them. This linkage between people and the places with which they are associated is a fundamental principle throughout the novel and, being perceived through the mind of the Narrator, it is constantly projected in sharp focus for the reader.

As far as the places encountered in the novel are concerned, the reader has no hard task here. I have already remarked that Paris is the central location for much of the novel: significantly, the undeniable reality of the capital is counterbalanced by two localities which are fictional: Combray and Balbec. To complete the list, only two other places are briefly visited: the fictional barracks-town of Doncières, and Venice. Thus in the very limited number of places which the novel inhabits one can perceive the interplay of reality and fiction at the most basic of levels: equal status is accorded to 'real' places and to 'unreal' ones, so much so that, distinctions between the two being blurred, it becomes meaningless to establish any difference. Hence Balbec can be quite as real as Paris, and Paris quite as fictional as Combray, such is the imaginative transformational power of art.

Combray

Combray is the first place one encounters in the novel (yet even here it is implicitly presented from the perspective of Paris). Actually, one encounters it twice, just as the Narrator attempts to recall it: first, in a false start, then in an exuberant, expansive version. The false start arises because the Narrator is relying on 'voluntary memory' – what it is possible to remember just as an intellectual exercise, and that is precious little. Here, all he can recall is a few rooms in the house where he and his family used to spend their summer holidays, 'comme si Combray n'avait consisté qu'en deux étages reliés par un mince escalier, et comme s'il n'y avait jamais été que sept heures du soir' (I, p.43). The only colour in these grey memories is provided by the brilliant projections of a magic lantern. As one would expect, the number of characters in this section is restricted to the immediate family, with one important exception: a certain Monsieur Swann, one of whose visits to the family results in a mighty psychological blow for the young Narrator, when his mother refuses to leave the visitor in order to impart the customary goodnight kiss ('il me fallut partir sans viatique', I, p.27).

Here the occasion of anguish, the mother unwittingly becomes the purveyor of intense joy when, many years later, she offers him a cup of tea and a madeleine cake. Upon tasting them, his mournful state is utterly transformed: 'Un plaisir délicieux m'avait envahi, isolé, sans la notion de sa cause [...] J'avais cessé de me sentir médiocre, contingent, mortel' (I, p.44). This is a 'moment bienheureux', one of those quasi-mystical experiences which, unheralded, visit the Narrator from time to time, and make him vividly aware that the humdrum confines of everyday life can be transcended. Here, it is the totality of his childhood in Combray which is resurrected, so that, just like Japanese papier-mâché water-flowers, 'toutes les fleurs de notre jardin et celles du parc de M. Swann, et les nymphéas de la Vivonne, et les bonnes gens du village et leurs petits logis et l'église et tout Combray et ses environs, tout cela qui prend forme et solidité, est sorti, ville et jardins, de ma tasse de thé' (I, p.47).

'Forme et solidité': it is emphatically not some woolly experience or vague feeling. On the contrary, specificity and a real sense of presence characterise such occasions. Hence the vividness with which Combray and its inhabitants are now evoked: an inspired 140 pages, crammed with incident and personalities. The contrast with the lacklustre description of Combray by voluntary memory could scarcely be more striking. A further contrast: whereas the first attempt at recall is shot through with a sense of irretrievable loss, the section resulting from the tasting of the madeleine possesses a completeness and an immediacy which prove that the seemingly impossible can happen, and time can be bridged effortlessly. So overwhelmingly present is the feeling produced by total recall that no space is left for the temporal difference which might allow room for nostalgia (though there is a degree of wistfulness in the final pages). In this way, Combray becomes an autonomous base on which to build, both as far as the Narrator is concerned, and as far as the other characters are also.

A famous, and readily discernible, feature of the Combray section of *Du côté de chez Swann* is the way in which the people are associated by the Narrator with one of two geographical locations. These are the country walks he and his family take in different directions, one towards Méséglise (Swann's way), the other towards Guermantes. Indeed, so important are the walks that they provide the name for two of the novel's seven named volumes. Each location is individually characterised and, by virtue of the separate point of the compass it inhabits, considered incompatible with the other. Thus the côté de Méséglise is associated with the bourgeois Swann and his immediate relations, notably his wife Odette and daughter Gilberte. The côté de Guermantes, on the other hand, leads the Narrator towards loftier realms, inhabited by the aristocratic family of that name.

The distinction between the two ways is so persistent in the Narrator's mind – it seems as if they exist in hermetically-sealed compartments of his brain – that it is not until shortly before the end of the novel that he learns from Gilberte, with whom he is staying near Combray, that the feat of combining them can easily be achieved:

> 'Si vous voulez, nous pourrons tout de même sortir un après-midi et nous pourrons alors aller à Guermantes, en prenant par Méséglise, c'est la plus jolie façon', phrase qui en bouleversant toutes les idées de mon enfance m'apprit que les deux côtés n'étaient pas aussi inconciliables que j'avais cru. (IV, p.268)

The 'côtés' are in some ways symbolic of what the Narrator sees as irreconcilable social strata; but the point is that ever since he convinced himself of this separateness, they never ceased to mix with one another, and to merge in various combinations. The realisation of geographical proximity essentially does no more than cap the social changes which the Narrator has been witnessing all the time since his youth.

The 'forme et solidité' of Combray is perhaps best summed up in the shape of its church, 'un édifice occupant, si l'on peut dire, un espace à quatre dimensions – la quatrième étant celle du Temps' (I, p.60). Its roots, like the people's, lie deep down in time, and it has been a continuing force for stability over the centuries, with 'sa tour qui avait contemplé saint Louis et semblait le voir encore' (I, p.61). But it is also 'Familière; mitoyenne, [...] simple citoyenne de Combray qui aurait pu avoir son numéro dans la rue si les rues de Combray avaient eu des numéros' (I, pp.61-62). And just as the concept of the 'deux côtés' will remain a constant feature of the Narrator's patterns of thought as he develops, so Combray church, in its unpretentiousness, will keep discreet company with him, and provide a ready point of reference, even at one of the most theoretical points of *Le Temps retrouvé*:

> Alors, je pensai tout d'un coup que si j'avais encore la force d'accomplir mon œuvre, cette matinée – comme autrefois à Combray certains jours qui avaient influé sur moi – qui m'avait, aujourd'hui même, donné à la fois l'idée de mon œuvre et la crainte de ne pouvoir la

> réaliser, marquerait certainement avant tout, dans celle-
> ci, la forme que j'avais pressentie autrefois dans l'église
> de Combray, et qui nous reste habituellement invisible,
> celle du Temps. (IV, pp.621-22)

So the church's backwards and forwards trajectory in time serves,
amongst many other things, as a model for the work of art upon
which the Narrator is to embark, and within which it is itself to be
enshrined.

A similar cultural model – but treated at first in a more frivolous manner – is appealed to in the shape of the *Arabian Nights*.
Amongst the crockery at Combray is a set of plates decorated with
scenes from that work; they are a particular favourite of the
Narrator's hypochondriac aunt Léonie, and she takes great pleasure
in looking at the pictures of Ali-Baba and Aladdin (I, p.56). But the
theme grows into something more serious when the Narrator
explicitly links these plates to the image of Combray church:

> Dans le gris et champenois Combray, leurs vignettes
> s'encastraient multicolores, comme dans la noire Eglise
> les vitraux aux mouvantes pierreries, comme dans le
> crépuscule de ma chambre les projections de la lanterne
> magique. (II, p.258)

This trilogy of images will subsist – like the notion of Combray
itself – all through the Narrator's career, and will notably resurface
at the end of *Le Temps retrouvé*, where they play a clinching
structural role. The *Arabian Nights* plates seem unlikely candidates,
but as so often in Proust new dimensions of earlier images are
subsequently revealed – here, the Narrator pictures himself in the
perilous position of Sheherezade *vis-à-vis* his own literary
production.

Paris

Paris provides a complete contrast to Combray. Although it contains
magical corners of its own, it has little of the village's spontaneous

character. And of course Paris is a real place about which everyone knows a lot, so there is no need for Proust to lend it an especially poetic presentation, or even present it at all. The name alone contains its own cultural and social associations which can be taken as read. Art, in particular, is what the precocious Narrator seeks out, and potential access to one of its branches, the theatre, is readily provided in the shape of one of the most distinctive features of the Paris landscape, the 'colonnes Morris' on which theatre posters are displayed. They become emblematic of his artistic desires, and set his imagination to work:

> Tous les matins je courais jusqu'à la colonne Morris pour voir les spectacles qu'elle annonçait. Rien n'était plus désintéressé et plus heureux que les rêves offerts à mon imagination par chaque pièce annoncée et qui étaient conditionnés à la fois par les images inséparables des mots qui en composaient le titre et aussi de la couleur des affiches encore humides et boursouflées de colle sur lesquelles il se détachait.
> (I, pp.72-73; cf. I, p.436)

This early enthusiasm for the theatre sets in train a whole sequence of artistic encounters for which Paris is the setting: literature, painting and music are appropriately given a capital place in the capital city.

But the Paris sections of *A la recherche du temps perdu* are probably most memorable for the social life which they contain. Here, the *Belle Epoque* is evoked in inimitable fashion. The huge middle volumes of the novel in particular see the Narrator becoming involved with a wide variety of characters in ever more glittering circles. He acts out a kind of social apprenticeship which takes him from humble beginnings to considerable heights. These volumes are punctuated by vast tableaux of society receptions, mainly hosted by the members of the Guermantes family. Although frivolity and superficiality seem to be the order of the day, more serious preoccupations emerge which indicate to the Narrator that much lies beneath the surface. These are human beings like any others, capable of self-deception, treachery, pomposity, delicacy, passion, cruelty – a whole range of emotions, values and activities which render them a microcosm of human behaviour in general.

At the same time, the Narrator's life in Paris is curiously continuous with his life in Combray. The family unit is ever-present and in close focus, and importantly the servant Françoise is brought up from Combray to the city. One of the most durable characters in the novel, her person physically links the two localities, and she alone survives to assist the Narrator in his literary task at the end of *Le Temps retrouvé*.

Before this event, the character of Paris changes noticeably for the Narrator: his life-style has undergone a major alteration, occasioned by his infatuation with Albertine. It is an unhealthy relationship, characterised by suspicion and jealousy: the very title *La Prisonnière* speaks volumes on this score. And while the affair does not preclude the normal round of socialising, it does mark a descent into morbid claustrophobia which will have serious repercussions on the Narrator's mental health. Altogether typical of his state of depression is this occasion when

> en levant une dernière fois mes yeux du dehors vers la fenêtre de la chambre dans laquelle je serais tout à l'heure, il me sembla voir le lumineux grillage qui allait se refermer sur moi et dont j'avais forgé moi-même, pour une servitude éternelle, les inflexibles barreaux d'or. (III, p.834)

As he says, he is caught in a prison of his own making, a vicious circle formed from a desire for total possession of Albertine – a possession which includes every detail of her past (did she ever know so-and-so? is she really a lesbian?) – an aim which he knows it is impossible to fulfil, and which, after her accidental death, becomes an almost pathological obsession.

Still, he eventually gets over all this, only to witness Paris totally transformed by the outbreak of war. A sustained parallel is made with the inhabitants of Pompeii upon the eruption of Vesuvius:

> Quelques-uns même de ces Pompéiens sur qui pleuvait déjà le feu du ciel descendirent dans les couloirs du métro, noirs comme des catacombes. Ils savaient en effet n'y être pas seuls. (IV, p.413)

War brings out a hidden, sensual side to people – perhaps occasioned by the proximity of death – which some of the darker pages of *Le Temps retrouvé* chronicle, including horrendous scenes in a male brothel (IV, pp.390 ff.). Altogether, Paris and its populace take on an alternately dream-like and apocalyptic appearance (parallels here are drawn with, yet again, the *Arabian Nights*, and with Wagner's music: IV, pp.411, 338). There is a funny side to it too, as when Saint-Loup and the Narrator invent newspaper society-column entries recording an evacuation: ' "Reconnu: la duchesse de Guermantes superbe en chemise de nuit, le duc de Guermantes inénarrable en pyjama rose et peignoir de bain" ' (IV, p.338).

Balbec

A holiday trip to the resort of Balbec on the Normandy coast is already mooted in the Combray period. Legrandin, the local snob and would-be socialite, has a sister who lives there, and he pompously expatiates on its beauties: 'Balbec! la plus antique ossature géologique de notre sol, vraiment Ar-mor, la Mer, la fin de la terre' (I, p.129). The antiquity of the place (like that of Combray church) instantly appeals to the young Narrator, and from now on he never ceases to fantasise about it. Later on Florence and Venice are added to Balbec as possible holiday destinations, providing an agreeably poetic trio for his imagination to play on. Balbec acquires even more prestige in his mind when his hero Swann exclaims: ' "Je crois bien que je connais Balbec! L'église de Balbec, du XIIe et XIIIe siècle, encore à moitié romane, est peut-être le plus curieux échantillon du gothique normand, et si singulière, on dirait de l'art persan" ' (I, pp.377-78). The artistic ingredient clinches it:

henceforth, Balbec becomes a veritable historico-cultural icon for the Narrator.

For reasons of illness, the journey is put off, but it does eventually take place, in the company of the grandmother and Françoise. The young Narrator's fantasy of taking the 'beau train généreux d'une heure vingt-deux' (I, p.378) is at last realised, and the trip into mythical lands actually occurs. But by dint of mythologising the place excessively, reality proves to be a disappointment. Intent on seeing what he has convinced himself is the reality – a cliff-like church beaten by sea-spray – the Narrator's dismay is complete when he discovers that it 'se dressait sur une place où était l'embranchement de deux lignes de tramways, en face d'un Café qui portait, écrit en lettres d'or, le mot "Billard"' (II, p.19). He tries to appreciate the statuary, but with little success: his apprenticeship in art still has a long way to go.

Apart from this initial setback – and most untypically for the Narrator – not much goes wrong with the stay. He greatly appreciates the natural beauty of the place, the amenities (and surprising poetry) of the Grand-Hôtel, and above all he meets people and makes new friends. In short, the stay at Balbec represents the archetypal holiday experience. The hotel in particular is a little world of its own, presenting 'toute une frise de personnages de guignol sortis de cette boîte de Pandore qu'était le Grand-Hôtel' (II, p.26). The guests all have their own idiosyncrasies, which the Narrator records in great detail (there are many excellent examples of Proust's famed qualities of observation).

But the Narrator's most significant encounters are less with inhabitants of the hotel than with outsiders: indeed, these people will play the most decisive roles in his future life. The first of them is Robert de Saint-Loup, the nephew of Mme de Villeparisis, an old schoolfriend of the Narrator's grandmother and a fellow-guest met again by accident. Saint-Loup is a veritable Adonis-figure, full of life and movement:

> Une après-midi de grande chaleur [...] je vis, grand,
> mince, le cou dégagé, la tête haute et fièrement portée,

> passer un jeune homme aux yeux pénétrants et dont la
> peau était aussi blonde et les cheveux aussi dorés que
> s'ils avaient absorbé tous les rayons du soleil. [...] Ses
> yeux, de l'un desquels tombait à tout moment un
> monocle, étaient de la couleur de la mer. (II, p.88)

The constantly dropping monocle becomes a leitmotiv indicative of
Saint-Loup's vivacity and impulsiveness, qualities much appreciated
by the Narrator, who is distinctly lacking in this respect. They make
a complementary pair, and remain great friends right up to Robert's
death in the war.

An uncle of Saint-Loup's is next to put in an appearance,
perceived by the Narrator in much the same fashion:

> Le lendemain matin [...] comme je passais seul
> devant le casino en rentrant à l'hôtel, j'eus la sensation
> d'être regardé par quelqu'un qui n'était pas loin de moi.
> Je tournai la tête et j'aperçus un homme d'une
> quarantaine d'années, très grand et assez gros, avec des
> moustaches très noires, et qui, tout en frappant
> nerveusement son pantalon avec une badine, fixait sur
> moi des yeux dilatés par l'attention. (II, p.110)

The penetrating eyes clearly run in the family: these especially
become the leitmotiv of the Baron de Charlus, for this is he. In
actual fact, the Narrator – and the reader – have come across them
before, way back in Combray days: there, in Swann's park, 'un
monsieur habillé de coutil et que je ne connaissais pas, fixait sur
moi des yeux qui lui sortaient de la tête' (I, p.140). This is an
excellent example of Proust's structuring over vast areas of space
and time. Charlus rapidly turns out to be a larger-than-life
character, full of inconsistencies, outrageous and opinionated, angry
and tender by turns. His massive presence dominates large parts of
the central volumes of the novel.

Equally dominant, but in a less flamboyant, more insidious
way, will be Albertine, who stands out for the Narrator from a group

of initially indistinguishable boisterous young girls, always up to
pranks. Little does he suspect at this stage what tragic consequences
will result from the affair he is about to have with her. What seems
to attract him is her very mystery, the difficulty he experiences in
perceiving her with any degree of stability: 'chaque fois,' he says,
'elle devait me sembler différente' (II, p.212). If there is one thing
about Albertine that is durable, it is her very changeability: she is
forever slipping out of the Narrator's mental reach.

Ironically, the person who formally introduces Albertine to
him represents the opposite pole of attraction, and a seemingly incompatible one: Elstir the painter. The uneasy cohabitation of love
and art is one of the major undercurrents of *A la recherche du temps
perdu*. As for Elstir in this instance, the Narrator's commentaries
are lofty and reverential:

> L'atelier d'Elstir m'apparut comme le laboratoire d'une
> sorte de nouvelle création du monde. [...] Au moment où
> j'entrais, le créateur était en train d'achever, avec le
> pinceau qu'il tenait dans sa main, la forme du soleil à
> son coucher. [...] Le charme de chacune [de ses marines]
> consistait en une sorte de métamorphose des choses
> représentées, analogue à celle qu'en poésie on nomme
> métaphore et que si Dieu le Père avait créé les choses en
> les nommant, c'est en leur ôtant leur nom, ou en leur en
> donnant un autre qu'Elstir les recréait. (II, pp.190-91)

The appreciation is altogether typical of the awe in which the
Narrator holds the arts in general: it is, of course, a condition to
which he himself aspires. 'Les rares moments où l'on voit la nature
telle qu'elle est, poétiquement, c'était de ceux-là qu'était faite
l'œuvre d'Elstir' (II, p.192). This ability of art to penetrate to the
heart of things, poetically, is invoked in these pages with singular
felicity, and many readers of *A l'ombre des jeunes filles en fleurs*
will have retained an impression of sustained poetry on Proust's
part: the whole tenor of life at Balbec is a lyrical one.

Venice

The Venice episode is only a brief one (about thirty pages), but it is placed at a significant juncture of the novel, and imparts a new impetus to the Narrator's life. For once, he fully appreciates the special artistic flavour of the city (unlike his experience of Balbec church: by now he is older and wiser), and is able to revel in its beauties. Of course, way back in *Du côté de chez Swann* he had indulged in fantasies about the place, realising that it was indeed possible, after an overnight train journey, to 's'éveiller le lendemain dans la cité de marbre et d'or "rehaussée de jaspe et pavée d'émeraudes" ' (I, p.385; the quote is from Ruskin – a typically second-hand artistic appreciation on the part of the young Narrator). Now, in *Albertine disparue*, his first-hand experience of Venice is one of aesthetic perfection and immediacy – perhaps engendered by the suddenness of the visit (he goes with his mother, at her suggestion).

Amongst many other artistic encounters, there is one with the paintings of Carpaccio. Earlier on, at the height of his affair with Albertine, the Narrator had bought her newly-fashionable dresses, created by the designer Fortuny (who based his work on old Venetian art), which 'faisaient apparaître [...] la Venise tout encombrée d'Orient où elles auraient été portées' (III, p.871). Now, actually in Venice himself, he is reminded of a day when Albertine

> avait jeté sur ses épaules un manteau de Fortuny qu'elle avait emporté avec elle le lendemain et que je n'avais jamais revu depuis dans mes souvenirs. Or c'était dans ce tableau de Carpaccio que le fils génial de Venise [Fortuny] l'avait pris, c'est des épaules de ce compagnon de la Calza qu'il l'avait détaché pour le jeter sur celles de tant de Parisiennes. (IV, p.226)

The memory fills him with melancholy, of course, but this feeling is 'bientôt dissipé' (ibid.). What remains, however, is the permanent reality of art in the face of human changeability and loss.

Another surprising reappearance – the Venice episode is full of surprises – is that of the *Arabian Nights*. Getting into a gondola, the Narrator feels as if 'la main mystérieuse d'un génie' is guiding him 'dans les détours de cette ville d'Orient' (IV, p.206). Later on, 'Le soir je sortais seul, au milieu de la ville enchantée où je me trouvais au milieu de quartiers nouveaux comme un personnage des *Mille et une Nuits*' (IV, p.229), a theme which is developed at some length, and which has come a considerable way – both geographically and aesthetically – from the scenes painted on Tante Léonie's plates back in Combray.

But the major lesson of the Venice episode is that Combray is, in reality, never very far away: just as 'il peut y avoir de la beauté, aussi bien que dans les choses les plus humbles, dans les plus précieuses – j'y goûtais des impressions analogues à celles que j'avais si souvent ressenties autrefois à Combray' (IV; p.202). Much space is devoted by the mature Narrator to demonstrating that 'à Venise [...] la vie quotidienne n'était pas moins réelle qu'à Combray' (IV, p.203). It is as if an overlapping of life and art is taking place: Combray was never before considered as an aesthetic whole, but now, given the experience of Venice, it can become one, just as the lofty artistic Venice can reveal its humble, down-to-earth dimension. And for the reader, this resurrection of Combray serves to induce the satisfying feeling that the novel is beginning to turn full-circle, and that the Narrator is not very far from his goal.

4. Comedy and Tragedy

Given the scope of *A la recherche du temps perdu*, it is scarcely surprising that characters are developed by Proust with a breadth and depth less readily attainable in more conventional novels. The full range of human emotions is explored, and this provides a veritable demonstration of the Pascalian 'grandeur et misère de l'homme'. Perhaps the most immediately visible manner in which these extremes are manifested is through the comic or tragic treatment which Proust gives them. There are wide variations of intensity, of course: sometimes the range is merely between humorous and sad. But at his most powerful, Proust scales the heights of comedy and plumbs the depths of tragedy.

Comedy

Nothing suffers more by being analysed than comedy, and with Proust this is particularly true, as knowledge of the wider context (even over several volumes) is frequently required. However, it should be possible to record, briefly, some notable incidents to prove that, in Maurice Bardèche's words, 'Proust est, avec Molière, le plus grand écrivain comique de notre langue, le plus imprévu, le plus profond, le plus riche en trouvailles de toutes sortes' (*18*, II, p.123).

We have already seen that the Narrator is a timid individual, accident-prone and generally unlucky; small surprise, then, that these negative attributes should provide a framework for potentially comic events. A good example occurs shortly after he arrives at the Grand-Hôtel in Balbec with his grandmother:

> Plus loin, derrière un vitrage clos, des gens étaient assis dans un salon de lecture pour la description duquel il m'aurait fallu choisir dans le Dante tour à tour les

> couleurs qu'il prête au Paradis et à l'Enfer, selon que je
> pensais au bonheur des élus qui avaient le droit d'y lire
> en toute tranquillité, ou à la terreur que m'eût causée
> ma grand-mère si dans son insouci de ce genre d'im-
> pressions, elle m'eût ordonné d'y pénétrer. (II, p.24)

The passage articulates the interplay of extremes mentioned above,
and in doing so in exalted terms (the comparisons with Dante)
points up the Narrator's intellectual precocity – easily made fun of –
and hence his vulnerability when faced with everyday situations.
Even though the crisis of being told to enter the reading-room does
not arise, its possibility is held, threateningly, in the air as the older
Narrator, tongue in cheek, relates the incident.

This vulnerability is there right from the earliest moments in
Combray, as, for example, when his fantasies about the duchesse de
Guermantes lead him to dream that, in the castle gardens, '[elle]
m'y faisait venir, éprise pour moi d'un soudain caprice; tout le jour
elle y pêchait la truite avec moi' (I, p.170). This ludicrous
proposition is just one of many manifestations of the same
syndrome: a massive disproportion between desire and reality,
totally unperceived by the over-serious younger Narrator. Still with
the duchesse de Guermantes, but much later on (in *Le Côté de
Guermantes*), the fantasies persist:

> J'aimais vraiment Mme de Guermantes. Le plus
> grand bonheur que j'eusse pu demander à Dieu eût été
> de faire fondre sur elle toutes les calamités, et que
> ruinée, déconsidérée, dépouillée de tous les privilèges
> qui me séparaient d'elle, n'ayant plus de maison où
> habiter ni de gens qui consentissent à la saluer, elle vînt
> me demander asile. Je l'imaginais le faisant. (II, p.367)

The comedy for the reader is a direct outcome of the Narrator's in-
ability to realise the absurdity of his fantasies. Indeed, the more
serious he is on this score, the funnier it is for the reader.

It is not just the older, wiser Narrator who realises that the young Narrator's personality sometimes makes him his own worst enemy. At Balbec, he is out walking with Elstir when the group of young girls whom he has noticed but not yet met draws up and engages in conversation with the artist, while the Narrator steps to one side in the expectation of being introduced:

> Mais déjà Elstir avait quitté les jeunes filles sans m'avoir appelé. Elles prirent une rue de traverse, il vint vers moi. Tout était manqué. [...] 'J'aurais été si content de les connaître', dis-je à Elstir en arrivant près de lui. 'Aussi pourquoi restez-vous à des lieues?'
>
> (II, pp.212, 215)

Elstir's no-nonsense attitude represents a salutary, but unheeded, counter to the Narrator's constant lack of practicality. In effect, the latter succeeds in creating the opposite state of affairs from that which he would wish, and in the process makes himself look ridiculous.

This tendency can even sometimes border on the catastrophic. After Albertine has left him, the Narrator is broken, and in desperation he persuades a little girl to come back to his apartment. All he does is rock her on his knees and give her 500 francs, but the parents find out and file a 'plainte en détournement de mineure' (IV, p.27). The court scene which ensues would be farcical but for the serious legal aspect: 'De mon innocence dans le fait il ne fut même pas question, car c'est la seule hypothèse que personne ne voulut admettre un instant' (ibid.). He gets off largely because the presiding 'chef de la Sûreté' likes little girls, and advises the Narrator to be more careful next time!

> Je sentais tellement qu'il ne me comprendrait pas si j'essayais de lui expliquer la vérité que je profitai sans mot dire de la permission qu'il me donna de me retirer. Tous les passants, jusqu'à ce que je fusse rentré, me parurent des inspecteurs chargés d'épier mes faits et gestes. (IV, p.28)

This final effect of alienation (so distressing for the Narrator, so amusing for the reader) seems to sum up the outcome which the Narrator's lack of contact with everyday reality so often provides. The whole affair is of his own making, and it so nearly turns out tragically; but seen in its wider context, both by the reader and by the older Narrator, the lasting impression of the incident is a comic one.

With most of the other characters in the novel, the situation is generally less extreme, though the production of humour is as often as not sparked off by the serious pretensions of the character in question. From a wealth of possible examples, I will choose two: the Narrator's aunt Léonie, and his schoolfriend Bloch. The priceless aunt Léonie takes her job as a professional hypochondriac very seriously indeed, lying in state overlooking the streets of Combray, and worrying when she sees a dog 'qu'elle ne connaissait point' (I, p.57). Her bedside table

> tenait à la fois de l'officine et du maître-autel; où, au-dessous d'une statuette de la Vierge et d'une bouteille de Vichy-Célestins, on trouvait des livres de messe et des ordonnances de médicaments, tout ce qu'il fallait pour suivre de son lit les offices et son régime, pour ne manquer l'heure ni de la pepsine, ni des Vêpres.
>
> (I, p.51)

In other words, the physical make-up of her situation and surroundings in itself creates the right conditions for humorous events: the incongruous juxtaposition of the religious statuette and the bottle of mineral-water is comically emblematic of this state of affairs, and becomes her own personal leitmotiv.

A common denominator in the production of comedy in Proust is that people unwittingly put themselves into positions which render them fair game for the Narrator's humorous attentions. Bloch, for instance, is overly fond of flowery language; arriving late for lunch, instead of excusing himself, he says:

'Je ne me laisse jamais influencer par les perturbations de l'atmosphère ni par les divisions conventionnelles du temps. Je réhabiliterais volontiers l'usage de la pipe d'opium et du kriss malais, mais j'ignore celui de ces instruments infiniment plus pernicieux et d'ailleurs platement bourgeois, la montre et le parapluie.' (I, p.91)

Not surprisingly, the Narrator's family are totally dismissive of such a pretentious youth, an attitude which is directly effected by the language Bloch employs and the attitudes it reveals. He never learns. Much later on in the novel, in *Le Côté de Guermantes*, he is at a reception given by Mme de Villeparisis; the latter is painting some flowers, surrounded by a few admirers, including an historian and Bloch:

> Bloch voulut faire un geste pour exprimer son admiration mais d'un coup de coude il renversa le vase où était la branche et toute l'eau se répandit sur le tapis.
> 'Vous avez vraiment des doigts de fée', dit à la marquise l'historien qui, me tournant le dos à ce moment-là, ne s'était pas aperçu de la maladresse de Bloch.
> Mais celui-ci crut que ces mots s'appliquaient à lui, et pour cacher sous une insolence la honte de sa gaucherie:
> 'Cela ne présente aucune importance, dit-il, car je ne suis pas mouillé.' (II, pp.512-13)

This time it is his eagerness to flatter which causes his downfall and renders him a figure of fun, precisely when he would wish to make a good impression.

Tragedy

The Narrator is for the most part an unlucky person. More than this, he also undergoes one truly tragic experience – tragic in the strict

sense of the term, for it is the direct result of a personal flaw. This is
the Albertine catastrophe. But before that, he will have had the
harrowing experience of his grandmother's final illness and death.
Here – and this is very different from the occasions of comedy – the
Narrator is not in a situation of his own making: on the contrary, he
is the powerless witness to an unfolding, inexorable drama.

It begins in the public toilets at the end of the Champs-Elysées
(they are there to this day); previously evoked in *A l'ombre des
jeunes filles en fleurs*, when Françoise hurriedly had to pay a call,
they were the backdrop to a barely-concealed sexual romp between
the Narrator and Gilberte (I. p.485). Now the picture is totally
different when his grandmother, emerging from them after a good
half hour, looking thoroughly shaken up, has clearly had 'une petite
attaque' (II, p.608). From now on, the progress of the illness unfolds
with the inevitability of Greek tragedy: indeed, the whole episode is
isolated in a brief chapter of its own (*Le Côté de Guermantes II*,
chapter I, about thirty pages long), thus emphasising its compressed
dramatic nature.

As if to underscore the drama, the chapter begins and ends
with references to Molière: not that the situation is comic, far from
it, but the irruption of out-of-place comedy renders the tragedy even
deeper. What makes it more poignant still is that the grandmother,
in an attempt to play down her condition, had herself half-quoted a
line from *Le Misanthrope* (II. p.607). And when a new doctor is
brought in as a last resort, it transpires that his name is as burlesque
as any invented by the famous dramatist: 'quand la servante disait
"M. Dieulafoy", on se croyait chez Molière' (II, p.638). Thus are
comedy and tragedy so intimately linked in the Narrator's world.

But there is precious little humour in the other major calamity
which hits him: the flight and subsequent death of Albertine. As I
have said, this is genuinely tragic, being the result of a flaw in his
character. That flaw is his obsession with the possibility of
obtaining total control over another person, total possession. He
believes that if he can find out every past act, motivation or thought
of Albertine's, then he can possess her in her entirety. Like so many
of his fantasies, it is of course unrealisable. What makes Albertine's

departure all the more brutal is the fact that the Narrator had slid into a sort of complacency, in which he had convinced himself that, having virtually imprisoned her in his flat, realisation of his dream of total possession was within his grasp. But he had failed to take into account the unexpected twists that habit ('l'Habitude', with a capital H) can take:

> Jusqu'ici je l'avais considérée surtout comme un pouvoir annihilateur qui supprime l'originalité et jusqu'à la conscience des perceptions; maintenant je la voyais comme une divinité redoutable, si rivée à nous, son visage insignifiant si incrusté dans notre cœur que si elle se détache, si elle se détourne de nous, cette déité que nous ne distinguions presque pas nous inflige des souffrances plus terribles qu'aucune et qu'alors elle est aussi cruelle que la mort. (IV, p.4)

But the suffering is really self-inflicted, for the Narrator, priding himself on having thought of every eventuality and catered for it, has clearly been guilty of the classical fault of hubris. It had never occurred to him that Albertine might take the initiative – *he* was to take all the decisions.

For the reader, the situation appears all the more vivid for the brisk handling it gets from Proust. It is a dramatic coup which rounds off *La Prisonnière*, in a hectic few lines when Françoise announces the news to a shattered Narrator ('mon souffle fut coupé, je tins mon cœur dans mes deux mains': III, p.915); and it forms an equally dramatic launching-point for *Albertine disparue*: '"Mademoiselle Albertine est partie!" Comme la souffrance va plus loin en psychologie que la psychologie!' (IV, p.3). So often criticised for long-windedness, Proust is incomparable at these moments of sudden reversal of fortunes.

Very many other characters in *A la recherche du temps perdu* experience such shifts in their situations, but I should like to single out the case of Swann: he is subject to especially poignant dramatic change and treatment. The whole of 'Un amour de Swann' could be

characterised as a study of human failure, so unsuccessful is Swann
in what he considers important (though appearing to others so
brilliant): his career acts as a cautionary tale for the Narrator,
though the latter rarely heeds its lessons. In the field of art, Swann
is a failure: he is knowledgeable and sensitive, yet cannot discipline
himself enough to complete a study of Vermeer he had started years
before (I, p.195). And in the rival field of love, his summing-up of
his affair with Odette (whom he is about to marry) is eloquent in its
dismissive self-accusation:

> 'Dire que j'ai gâché des années de ma vie, que j'ai voulu
> mourir, que j'ai eu mon plus grand amour, pour une
> femme qui ne me plaisait pas, qui n'était pas mon
> genre!' (I, p.375)

Very much as the Narrator will do, Swann has succeeded in
manœuvring himself into a position which is just the opposite of his
original intentions.

This is Swann's real tragedy (and it might also partially be the
Narrator's), that he cannot bring his desires to a successful
conclusion. Frivolous individuals such as the duc and duchesse de
Guermantes have a marvellous social life (which is all they seek),
but Swann, being built of sterner stuff, is constantly reminded of
unfulfilled aspirations. The two worlds come into direct conflict in a
memorable scene when the Guermantes couple, about to dash off to
a fashionable party, are engaging in hasty conversation with Swann,
who has paid a surprise visit. They want him to spend the spring
holidays in Italy with them, but he says it will probably be
impossible; when pressed for the reason, he simply says, 'Mais, ma
chère amie, c'est que je serai mort depuis plusieurs mois' (II,
p.882). Literally on the point of getting into her carriage, the
duchesse finds herself in a quandary:

> Placée pour la première fois de sa vie entre deux devoirs
> aussi différents que monter dans sa voiture pour aller
> dîner en ville, et témoigner de la pitié à un homme qui

va mourir, elle ne voyait rien dans le code des con-
venances qui lui indiquât la jurisprudence à suivre.

(II, p.882)

The way out she finds is to hope Swann is joking ('Vous voulez
plaisanter?'); but when it transpires that he isn't, the next few
minutes (two pages of text) are spent in a balancing act. Not
surprisingly, flippancy wins the day, and the Guermantes sweep off
to their society appointment, with the duc shouting to Swann: 'Vous
vous portez comme le Pont-Neuf. Vous nous enterrerez tous!' (II,
p.884). They are the last words of *Le Côté de Guermantes*, the
misplaced humour ironically underlining the tragedy of Swann's
position in a powerful conclusion.

M. de Charlus, the tragi-comic character par excellence

Apart from the Narrator, M. de Charlus probably encompasses a
wider range of human foibles, emotions, ups and downs, grandeur
and misery, than any other character in Proust's novel. To the
Narrator he is for a long while profoundly enigmatic, presenting
apparently contradictory personalities from one moment to the next.
His haughty demeanour when they first meet at Balbec conceals a
sensitive nature, one which is easily hurt – but which can equally be
used to hurt others. He specialises in pouring scorn on others in
devastating one-liners. After deploring in no uncertain terms the
fact that a former residence of the Guermantes is now in the
possession of a Jewish family, his punch-line completes the
demolition:

> Cela fait penser à cette chambre du château de Blois où
> le gardien qui le faisait visiter me dit: 'C'est ici que
> Marie Stuart faisait sa prière; et c'est là maintenant où
> ce que je mets mes balais.' (II, p.123)

Nothing if not outrageous, he scandalises the Narrator by pinching
him and exclaiming 'Mais on s'en fiche bien de sa vieille grand-

mère, hein? petite fripouille!' (II. 126); but when the latter protests
his adoration of his grandmother. Charlus upbraids him. He, the
Narrator, should show greater maturity, and thereby avoid having
'l'air de parler à tort et à travers comme un sourd et d'ajouter par là
un second ridicule à celui d'avoir des ancres brodées sur votre
costume· de bain' (ibid.). Charlus is a master at such sleights of
expression which enable him to make others feel foolish and ensure
his tactical superiority.

When he is in full flow, his humour can be devastating. In
Sodome et Gomorrhe, frequenting the Verdurins' salon for a while
(normally, he would consider it beneath him, but his latest boy-
friend, Morel, plays the violin for them), he cannot resist launching
side-swipes of breathtaking insolence. Thus, when he tells Madame
Verdurin of his plans to celebrate his patron saint Michael's day at
the Mont-Saint-Michel, and she half-heartedly asks 'Ça vous
intéresse beaucoup, ces affaires-là?', he launches the most crushing
of ripostes: 'Vous êtes peut-être affligée de surdité intermittente. [...]
Je vous ai dit que saint Michel était un de mes glorieux patrons' (III,
p.347). And he is supposed to be her guest!

But even before this he had firmly put the Verdurins in their
place. They, unaware that Charlus eccentrically uses his lowest title
of baron even though he possesses higher ones, unwittingly fall into
a trap which will enable him to humiliate them. At dinner, they
have given precedence in the seating arrangements to a marquis,
and upon a slight remonstrance on Charlus's part, M. Verdurin
starts to explain:

> 'Mais enfin puisqu'il y avait justement M. de
> Cambremer et qu'il est marquis, comme vous n'êtes que
> baron ... – Permettez, répondit M. de Charlus avec un
> air de hauteur, à M. Verdurin étonné, je suis aussi duc
> de Brabant, damoiseau de Montargis, prince d'Oléron,
> de Carency, de Viareggio et des Dunes. D'ailleurs cela
> ne fait absolument rien. Ne vous tourmentez pas',
> ajouta-t-il en reprenant son fin sourire, qui s'épanouit

> sur ces derniers mots: 'J'ai tout de suite vu que vous
> n'aviez pas l'habitude.' (III, p.333)

This is virtuoso stuff indeed, a wit at the devastating height of his powers.

But it is not to last. In *La Prisonnière*, at a Verdurin reception similar in every respect to the one where we have just seen Charlus triumph over his hosts, the operation goes into reverse and the tables are turned in comprehensive fashion. The Verdurins have managed to persuade Morel that Charlus has evil intentions towards him and have mobilised him in their favour, and against his self-elected Maecenas:

> 'Laissez-moi, je vous défends de m'approcher, cria
> Morel au baron. Vous ne devez pas être à votre coup
> d'essai, je ne suis pas le premier que vous essayez de
> pervertir!' Ma seule consolation était de penser que
> j'allais voir Morel et les Verdurin pulvérisés par M. de
> Charlus. Pour mille fois moins que cela j'avais essuyé
> ses colères de fou, personne n'était à l'abri d'elles, un
> roi ne l'eût pas intimidé. Or il se produisit cette chose
> extraordinaire. On vit M. de Charlus, muet, stupéfait,
> mesurant son malheur sans en comprendre la cause, ne
> trouvant pas un mot, levant les yeux successivement sur
> toutes les personnes présentes, d'un air interrogateur,
> indigné, suppliant, et qui semblait leur demander moins
> encore ce qui s'était passé que ce qu'il devait répondre.
>   (III, p.820)

For once Charlus can find no words to express his feelings: it is a contingency he has never known, a scene for which he has never needed to rehearse. Yet, like the Narrator, he is instrumental in preparing his own downfall: he possesses his own brand of hubris, the expectation that he will always be on top of any given situation. When, as here, he is not, he has no response, and is vulnerable to attack from a person who has learned a lesson or two in invective from him.

From this point, M. de Charlus's career is all downhill, but not without that grandeur which had always been his. So, when the Narrator, having strayed by chance into a male brothel during the wartime blackout, peeks through a side window,

> là, enchaîné sur un lit comme Prométhée sur son rocher, recevant les coups d'un martinet en effet planté de clous que lui infligeait Maurice, je vis, déjà tout en sang, et couvert d'ecchymoses qui prouvaient que le supplice n'avait pas lieu pour la première fois, je vis devant moi M. de Charlus. (IV, p.394)

The scene may be as degrading as one could imagine, but the parallel the Narrator draws with an illustrious tragic figure (all the more authoritative for being mythical) confers on Charlus a certain sort of dignity which transcends the unedifying position in which he has placed himself.

He is practically in his dotage, but remains magnificent, with the Narrator sustaining the tragic tenor in the most flattering of comparisons, seeing in this 'vieux prince déchu la majesté d'un roi Lear' (IV, p.438; see also p.501). He can even rise in dramatic fashion to give glimpses of his former powers of oratory. At his last appearance in *Le Temps retrouvé* he harangues the Narrator as only he knows how, in a soliloquy on his dead friends:

> C'est avec une dureté presque triomphale qu'il répétait sur un ton uniforme, légèrement bégayant et aux sourdes résonances sépulcrales: 'Hannibal de Bréauté, mort! Antoine de Mouchy, mort! Charles Swann, mort! Adalbert de Montmorency, mort! Boson de Talleyrand, mort! Sosthène de Doudeauville, mort!' Et chaque fois, ce mot 'mort' semblait tomber sur ces défunts comme une pelletée de terre plus lourde, lancée par un fossoyeur qui tenait à les river plus profondément à la tombe. (IV, p.441)

As a macabre example of Charlus's theatricality, this could hardly be bettered. But it is more than this: we have seen how, in his prime, he had crushed the Verdurins with a mere list of his titles; now the selfsame technique of enumeration is employed, this time to a more gloomy end. The dramatic symmetry of the two scenes is clear enough, as striking as the symmetry between his victory over the Verdurins and theirs over him. In sum, Charlus's career is nothing if not dramatic: for this tragi-comic genius, the world is literally a stage.

5. The Failure of Love

The Proustian definition of love is grim. For a novel which is in many ways so optimistic, which celebrates life in no uncertain fashion, *A la recherche du temps perdu* is at its most pessimistic when dealing with the traditionally positive experience of love. The attitude towards love within the novel is of course the Narrator's; but because of the particular force with which the analysis is presented one cannot help but feel that this is especially close to Proust's own voice. There may or may not be true autobiographical reasons for such a state of affairs, but there is a formal, structural feature of the novel which guarantees and explains this force.

There are two great love-affairs in the novel: Swann and Odette, the Narrator and Albertine. The latter is presented within the framework of the Narrator's own *Bildungsroman*; but the former is presented outside of the framework, as a self-enclosed short story. Importantly, that story is placed very early in the unfolding of the Narrator's life (in fact, it predates his birth: see I, p.184); in this way, it can be held in mind, both by the Narrator and by the reader, as a cautionary tale. More importantly, the story is narrated in the third person, thus being freed from the fluid subjectivity which first-person narration might have permitted, and achieving a certain objectivity. Most important, though, is the fact that the narrating individual is consubstantial with the Narrator of the main body of the novel, thus carrying in his person simultaneous commitment and detachment – commitment because we know of his interest in Swann and his family, detachment because he was uninvolved in anything that is recounted. What this unique situation of the Narrator in 'Un amour de Swann' permits (and which first-person narration would have precluded) is the possibility of judgement. And that judgement is damning.

The Case of Swann

We have already seen what Swann's verdict on his affair with
Odette will be ('Dire que j'ai gâché des années de ma vie [...]': I,
p.375). But we could already guess this from the very title 'Un
amour de Swann': the dismissive 'un' speaks volumes about the
ephemeral nature of love as the Narrator sees it. Indeed, the
impression one gets from a reading of 'Un amour de Swann' is that
of a ruthless analytical mind applying itself to a specimen presented
for dissection. This mind has clear-cut opinions about love, and
speaks with a voice sharpened by experience:

> A l'âge déjà un peu désabusé dont approchait Swann et
> où l'on sait se contenter d'être amoureux pour le plaisir
> de l'être sans trop exiger de réciprocité, ce rap-
> prochement des cœurs, s'il n'est plus comme dans la
> première jeunesse le but vers lequel tend nécessairement
> l'amour, lui reste uni en revanche par une association
> d'idées si forte qu'il peut en devenir la cause, s'il se
> présente avant lui. Autrefois on rêvait de posséder le
> cœur de la femme dont on était amoureux; plus tard,
> sentir qu'on possède le cœur d'une femme peut suffire à
> vous en rendre amoureux. (I, p.193)

The language seems measured, but it carries with it an authority
which brooks no contradiction – the frequent use of 'on' and the
tendency towards maxim-style constructions ensure this.

These are *ex cathedra* pronouncements, and they grow ever
more incisive as they stud the depressing story of Swann and
Odette:

> De tous les modes de production de l'amour, de
> tous les agents de dissémination du mal sacré, il est bien
> l'un des plus efficaces, ce grand souffle d'agitation qui
> parfois passe sur nous. Alors l'être avec qui nous nous

> plaisons à ce moment-là. le sort en est jeté, c'est lui que
> nous aimerons. (I. p.227)

The sly introduction of the first person plural allows the Narrator
the possibility of moving effortlessly between the particular and the
general, using Swann's predicament as one for general applicability,
and at the same time branding the supposed emotion with a
damning label. Even if love does exist, it is not a simple entity:

> Car ce que nous croyons notre amour, notre jalousie,
> n'est pas une même passion continue, indivisible. Ils se
> composent d'une infinité d'amours successifs, de
> jalousies différentes et qui sont éphémères, mais par leur
> multitude ininterrompue donnent l'impression de la
> continuité, l'illusion de l'unité. (I, p.366)

In a formulation worthy of La Rochefoucauld, jealousy is given
equal status to love; indeed. it is inseparable from it, as the
syntactical contiguity (it is a form of parataxis) twice graphically
demonstrates. And this major fragmentation of what seemed to be a
monolithic unit opens up a whole process of infinite fragmentation,
hence destabilisation.

    'L'illusion de l'unité': this sums up so much of Swann's –
hence 'our' – attitude towards love, looking for highly elusive
substance. In the Narrator's eyes. love is so often a case of self-
persuasion, the creation of a state of affairs from a received, but
unproven, notion. Certainly. this is the case with Swann who,
persuading himself of the value of his love, fabricates a whole
mythology with which to endow it with life. So, famously, Odette
'frappa Swann par sa ressemblance avec cette figure de Zéphora, la
fille de Jéthro. qu'on voit dans une fresque de la chapelle Sixtine' (I,
p.219). Given Swann's artistic temperament, such a reaction comes
as little surprise; but where, for the Narrator. he sins is by inverting
the respective values of art and life. debasing the former in order to
elevate the latter:

> Il plaça sur sa table de travail, comme une
> photographie d'Odette, une reproduction de la fille de
> Jéthro. [...] Quand il avait regardé longtemps ce
> Botticelli, il pensait à son Botticelli à lui qu'il trouvait
> plus beau encore et, approchant de lui la photographie
> de Zéphora, il croyait serrer Odette contre son cœur.
>
> (I, pp.221-22)

What, in effect, Swann is doing here is seeking – and of course
finding – an ingenious outlet for his love, creating a personal
illusion. The case is identical with the Vinteuil violin sonata, whose
'petite phrase [...] était comme l'air national de leur amour' (I,
p.215): they appropriate it, not for its intrinsic musical worth, but as
a lofty validation of their imagined love.

Even sexual intercourse becomes gratuitously beautified in
this general rush for substitutes. Its first occurrence followed on
from Swann's rearranging a spray of orchids (the variety called
'catleya') on Odette's corsage; from then on, in their personal
mythology, 'faire catleya' is the term they always employ for
making love. But note the whiplash applied by the Narrator in
conveying this information:

> Bien plus tard, quand l'arrangement (ou le simulacre
> rituel d'arrangement) des catleyas fut depuis longtemps
> tombé en désuétude, la métaphore 'faire catleya',
> devenue une simple vocable qu'ils employaient sans y
> penser quand ils voulaient signifier l'acte de la
> possession physique – où d'ailleurs l'on ne possède rien
> – survécut dans leur langage, où elle le commémorait, à
> cet usage oublié. (I, p.230)

Ruthless in his pithy aside, the Narrator, in typically jaundiced
mood, effectively pronounces a global denial of received opinion
(the 'on' again), perhaps the most damning of all that punctuate
'Un amour de Swann'. And as far as Swann is concerned, this

maxim points up just what a gulf exists between the mature, experienced Narrator and the supposed man of the world Swann, who here demonstrates just how foolish the most sophisticated person can be: it will take him another 150 pages to catch up with the Narrator and realise that Odette 'n'était pas [s]on genre!' (I, p.375).

The Case of the Narrator

Yet to the young Narrator, Swann is a hero, and the warning note sounded by his *alter ego* as omniscient narrator is as yet unavailable to him; but the fact of Swann's failure in love, however unclearly articulated, is there before him, and he will ignore it at his peril. Of course, this is just what he proceeds to do, with characteristic obtuseness. His relationship with Albertine is a sorry affair in all ways, and one which he constantly wishes he had never embarked upon. It follows a long and tortuous path and, as with so many things in the Narrator's life, it unfolds in a random, unpredictable fashion; only after it is all over is it possible to discern an overall pattern.

'Je savais maintenant que j'aimais Albertine' (II, p.278). With this admission, the Narrator has unwittingly embarked on his greatest, most time- and energy-consuming, most intense – and in the final analysis, most futile – adventure. Nothing very serious seems to be in the offing until his second stay at Balbec in *Sodome et Gomorrhe* (the first stay and subsequent meetings in Paris had been little more than flirtations). What really sets the affair going is not any positive connotations the word 'love' might possess, but seemingly negative concepts such as jealousy and suspicion.

He is suspicious above all that Albertine has had, indeed maybe still has, lesbian relationships; her tendency to be economical with the truth exacerbates this distrust. In spite of her protestations, the evidence is very clearly positive, but the Narrator requires both absolute proof of her full sexual orientation and an exhaustive list of those she has had affairs with. Neither is of course forthcoming. And even if it were, how would that be of any consolation to him?

What he in effect seeks is a means of arriving at total knowledge of another person, and in so doing exercising absolute control over her. He seems to imagine that revelations about her past are somehow tantamount to possession of that past: the more he knew, the more fully would he 'own' her. He could not be more wrong.

A particular obsession of his concerns Mlle Vinteuil, daughter of the Combray composer, and a friend of hers (ominously always called just 'l'amie de Mlle Vinteuil'). They are notorious lesbians, and the Narrator lives in constant apprehension that Albertine will get involved with them. So that, when she lets slip that she has known them for years, it is worse than anything he could have imagined. Ironically, she thinks the information will impress him, because of the musical connection (she doesn't realise he knows of their reputation). But for him, 'C'était une *terra incognita* terrible où je venais d'atterrir, une phase nouvelle de souffrances insoupçonnées qui s'ouvrait' (III, p.500). This discovery leads straight to a major decision which he announces to his mother in the resounding final words of *Sodome et Gomorrhe*: 'il faut absolument que j'épouse Albertine' (III, p.515). As if by marrying her he could annul her past misdemeanours, or somehow, by 'possessing' them, render them harmless. The venture is clearly doomed from the start.

But what we witness in *La Prisonnière* is in a way the projected marriage – today it would be called a trial marriage – with all the close-up detail that that would entail. Even though the affair has scarcely had an auspicious start, we do get an insight into the conflicting impulses within the Narrator's love for Albertine: her protracted stay in his apartment allows the reader prolonged contact with the continuity and intimacy of their domestic life. What the Narrator derives from having her close by him is 'un pouvoir d'apaisement tel que je n'avais pas éprouvé de pareil depuis les soirs lointains de Combray où ma mère penchée sur mon lit venait m'apporter le repos dans un baiser' (III, p.585). Mention of the magic word 'Combray' opens up a whole package of contentment with which we are abundantly familiar. So one should not under-estimate Albertine's charm; certainly there is something close to the idyllic about some of the scenes in *La Prisonnière*, as when she is asleep:

> Je sautais sans bruit sur le lit, je me couchais au long
> d'elle, je prenais sa taille d'un de mes bras, je posais
> mes lèvres sur sa joue et sur son cœur, puis sur toutes les
> parties de son corps posais ma seule main restée libre, et
> qui était soulevée aussi comme les perles, par la
> respiration d'Albertine; moi-même, j'étais déplacé
> légèrement par son mouvement régulier. Je m'étais
> embarqué sur le sommeil d'Albertine. (III, p.580)

There is no gainsaying the poetry of these evocations – such
apparently blissful moments of intimacy evidently mean a lot to the
Narrator – but the idyll is clearly based on false premises. Already,
the title of the volume tells what one of them is: the notion of
imprisonment is manifestly incompatible with lasting happiness.
Then again, the early pages are so riddled with negative
assessments of the situation ('Je n'aimais plus Albertine': III, p.530
– repeated twice within a page) and with ominous vocabulary
('jalousie' several times on III. pp.531-33) that it is impossible to
believe in contented domesticity for very long.

What, however, is most revelatory about the Narrator's relationship with Albertine is that the serenity is greatest when she is
asleep. In a rare burst of lucidity, he analyses the situation perfectly:

> Son sommeil réalisait dans une certaine mesure. la
> possibilité de l'amour: seul, je pouvais penser à elle,
> mais elle me manquait. je ne la possédais pas. Présente.
> je lui parlais, mais étais trop absent de moi-même pour
> pouvoir penser. Quand elle dormait. je n'avais plus à
> parler, je savais que je n'étais plus regardé par elle, je
> n'avais plus besoin de vivre à la surface de moi-même.
> [...] Elle s'était réfugiée, enclose, résumée, dans son
> corps. En le tenant sous mon regard. dans mes mains,
> j'avais cette impression de la posséder tout entière que je
> n'avais pas quand elle était réveillée. Sa vie m'était

soumise, exhalait vers moi son léger souffle. (III, p.578)

'J'avais cette impression' – a most attractive impression, certainly, but nevertheless a figment of the Narrator's imagination. In an attempt to impose some sort of stability on the 'être de fuite' that Albertine is (III, p.600), he is in effect lying to himself, thereby compounding her own lies which are 'si nombreux' (III, p.605). Watching her sleep is really an exercise in fantasy, an interlude from the direct task in hand – 'Ses mensonges, ses aveux, me laissaient à achever la tâche d'éclaircir la vérité' (ibid.) – a task he can never hope to complete.

If he imagines that by virtually imprisoning Albertine and subjecting her to cross-examination he can get at the truth, then not only is he fooling himself, but he is actually performing himself an immense disservice by ensuring his own 'esclavage à Paris' (III, p.873). Besides, the unhealthy nature of this claustrophobic relationship leads him into even poorer judgement, as when Albertine, playing the pianola, is described as 'cet ange musicien, œuvre d'art qui, tout à l'heure, par une douce magie, allait se détacher de sa niche et offrir à mes baisers sa substance précieuse et rose' (III, p.885). Is he falling into the same trap as Swann, by contaminating art and life? Aware of the possible parallel, he himself invokes the case of Swann, and forestalls negative comment: 'Mais non; Albertine n'était nullement pour moi une œuvre d'art' (ibid.). Is this really true? What about his descriptions of her asleep? By protesting too much, the Narrator is in effect inviting the comparison with Swann.

Albertine's subsequent flight and death in a riding accident unsurprisingly exacerbate his mental condition, resulting in a morbid resurrection of his obsession with her possible lesbian exploits. Grotesquely, he sends Aimé, the maître d'hôtel at Balbec, on a mission to find out whether she had had an affair with a certain laundry-girl, and has his suspicions confirmed (IV, pp.105-06). But where can such information get him now? She is dead, and his aim of total possession no longer has an object: yet the mechanism of inquisition goes on blindly, with a life of its own. As the Narrator

pertinently remarks, 'Pour que la mort d'Albertine eût pu supprimer
mes souffrances, il eût fallu que le choc l'eût tuée non seulement en
Touraine, mais en moi' (IV, p.60). Her afterlife is if anything even
more vivid for him as memories of many occasions come flooding
back uncontrollably.

Yet the suffering, similar to that which follows an amputation
(IV, p.73), subsides. The Narrator eloquently sets out the reason
why:

> Comme il y a une géométrie dans l'espace, il y a une
> psychologie dans le temps, où les calculs d'une
> psychologie plane ne seraient plus exacts parce qu'on
> n'y tiendrait pas compte du Temps et d'une des formes
> qu'il revêt, l'oubli; l'oubli dont je commençais à sentir
> la force et qui est un si puissant instrument d'adaptation
> à la réalité parce qu'il détruit peu à peu en nous le passé
> survivant qui est en constante contradiction avec elle. Et
> j'aurais vraiment bien pu deviner plus tôt qu'un jour je
> n'aimerais plus Albertine. (IV, p.137)

So in effect, everything goes into reverse: just as the Narrator's
relationship with Albertine was a process of agglutination in time,
so now the component parts gradually slip away as time passes.
Surprisingly rapid, the process leads the Narrator back from the
boundaries of insanity. Even when he receives a telegram
purporting to be from a resurrected Albertine (it is a mistake: a
telegraph employee had wrongly transcribed the real signatory's
name, Gilberte [Swann]: see IV, pp.234-35), he can remain totally
collected:

> Maintenant qu'Albertine dans ma pensée ne vivait plus
> pour moi, la nouvelle qu'elle était vivante ne me causa
> pas la joie que j'aurais cru. Albertine n'avait été pour
> moi qu'un faisceau de pensées, elle avait survécu à sa
> mort matérielle tant que ces pensées vivaient en moi; en
> revanche maintenant que ces pensées étaient mortes,

> Albertine ne ressuscitait nullement pour moi avec son
> corps. (IV, p.220)

In reducing the whole affair with Albertine to a matter of thought
alone, the Narrator could not provide a bleaker analysis of the
nature of love: it is an illusion. created in one's mind by dint of
belief in the abstract notion of it. The affair has been an enormous
waste of time and effort, in the service of a non-existent concept.
But an unexpected positivity results from the Narrator's by now
wide experience in this area: he is wiser and, unlike Swann, is now
free to embark on more fruitful paths.

6. The Triumph of Art

> En somme, dans un cas comme dans l'autre, qu'il s'agît
> d'impressions comme celle que m'avait donnée la vue
> des clochers de Martinville, ou de réminiscences comme
> celle de l'inégalité des deux marches ou le goût de la
> madeleine, il fallait tâcher d'interpréter les sensations
> comme les signes d'autant de lois et d'idées, en essayant
> de penser, c'est-à-dire de faire sortir de la pénombre ce
> que j'avais senti, de le convertir en un équivalent
> spirituel. Or, ce moyen qui me paraissait le seul,
> qu'était-ce autre chose que faire une œuvre d'art?
>
> (IV, p.457)

Before arriving at this key realisation, the Narrator will have had to undergo many trials and follow false paths before he is mentally – one might say spiritually – prepared for the arduous task which lies ahead. He has notably had to negotiate the minefield of love: as we have seen, it was a painful experience. But a purgative one too, for it has cleared his system of much wasteful material.

Ironically – or was it by some inscrutable design? – it is precisely his relationship with Albertine that will enable him to come into closer contact with art. Not that she was very artistic herself (though not lacking in culture), and she seems scarcely to have profited by her proximity to major artists. She is more of a social creature, and this is how we first witness her, when she is an acquaintance of Elstir's before the Narrator is. With Bergotte, the relationship is equally superficial, notably extending to her claiming to have had a conversation with the writer (this by way of concealing her real, suspect, activities) when in fact he was dying in dramatic circumstances, at an art exhibition. With Vinteuil, the relationship is of course the lesbian one with the composer's daughter and her infamous friend.

All of this is anecdotal, but it is precisely in its being so trivial, so humdrum, that its significance lies. For the reader, Albertine's close contact with great artists is a constant reminder of how the Narrator squanders his own considerable gifts on a worthless individual, and of how much better things would be for him if he were to profit by his artistic nature. In effect, Albertine's artistic contacts might be considered potential 'transfer-points' to art for the Narrator, would he only avail himself of them. But on this point, as on so many others, he follows his own slow rhythm. Perhaps the element of artistic procrastination represented by the affair with Albertine is in some way a prerequisite for eventual success in this field, an intellectual 'reculer pour mieux sauter', though at the time not perceived in such positive terms.

However this may be, one analysis is sure: the Narrator comes out of the affair with his illusions shattered, and although art as an ideal survives intact, what guarantee is there that it can play a meaningful part in his life? Will he ever be capable of realising his vocation? The question-marks accumulate apace, and the doubting persona re-emerges with a vengeance. But before seeing how the Narrator copes with this new challenge, we need to look at what art has meant for him up to this point – surely he is not going to jettison it all now?

Bergotte and Elstir

The writer Bergotte, like the other artists (and in common with all personages of significance), is firmly associated with a place, here Combray, and specifically with the time the Narrator spends reading him on the idle hill of summer. His writings express 'toute une philosophie nouvelle', they engender a 'chant de harpes', and clearly strike a chord with the Narrator on a deep level:

> Un de ces passages de Bergotte, le troisième ou le
> quatrième que j'eusse isolé du reste, me donna une joie

incomparable à celle que j'avais trouvée au premier, une
joie que je me sentis éprouver en une région plus
profonde de moi-même, plus unie, plus vaste, d'où les
obstacles et les séparations semblaient avoir été enlevés.

(I, p.93)

One recognises straight away the Narrator's characteristic
vocabulary of breadth and profundity to designate areas of
sensibility which he particularly cherishes: the words carry a
distinct accent of awe.

Even though his opinion of Bergotte lessens as he grows older
(the youthful enthusiasm clearly cannot last intact), the fictional
author's writings remain as a constant reference-point in the future.
Thus he is able to overcome his disappointment when M. de
Norpois, his father's pompous diplomat friend, dismissively labels
Bergotte 'un joueur de flûte' (I, p.464). And when he himself
actually meets the writer whom he imagines to be a 'doux Chantre
aux cheveux blancs', the latter turns out to be 'un homme jeune,
rude, petit, râblé et myope, à nez rouge en forme de coquille de
colimaçon et à barbiche noire' (I, p.537). Not surprisingly, the
Narrator is 'mortellement triste' at the collapse of his fantasy-
portrait of Bergotte. Yet, characteristically, he rallies, and by the
time of the writer's death (so shamefully sullied by Albertine's
lying), he has restored Bergotte to a position of glory. One of
Proust's most famous purple passages (a technique which,
incidentally, the Narrator much appreciates in Bergotte himself: see
I, p.94), it concludes with a suitably emphatic spiritual invocation:

On l'enterra, mais toute la nuit funèbre, aux
vitrines éclairées, ses livres, disposés trois par trois,
veillaient comme des anges aux ailes éployées et
semblaient pour celui qui n'était plus, le symbole de sa
résurrection. (III, p.693)

The Narrator's estimation of the painter Elstir follows very
much the same pattern as that of Bergotte: in chapter 3, I quoted a

passage indicating in what reverence he holds this 'artiste très connu, de grande valeur' (II, p.182). Enthusiasm dips when, visiting the painter for the first time, the Narrator notes that Elstir's villa 'était peut-être la plus somptueusement laide' of a new housing development (II, p.190). But he bounces back when in the studio, surrounded by paintings by 'le créateur' (ibid.): here he is in his element, existing as it were in a world of pure culture, perceived with no distracting intermediaries. Rapt attention takes hold of him, a sure sign of artistic communion:

> Une fois en tête à tête avec les Elstir, j'oubliai tout à fait l'heure du dîner; de nouveau comme à Balbec j'avais devant moi les fragments de ce monde aux couleurs inconnues qui n'était que la projection de la manière de voir particulière à ce grand peintre et que ne traduisaient nullement ses paroles. (II, p.712)

This quotation is taken not from the Balbec section of *A l'ombre des jeunes filles en fleurs*, but from *Le Côté de Guermantes*, when the Narrator's socialising is at its height; importantly, it shows how constant his response to Elstir is (here he is viewing the duc de Guermantes's collection), and displays his continuing faith in art in general, even at a time when one might imagine him to be most neglectful of it.

At the same time as providing a supreme artistic model, Elstir proves to be an invaluable pedagogical force too. As we saw in chapter 3, the Narrator is disappointed when he finally sees Balbec church: it fails to live up to his romantic fantasies. 'Comment,' exclaims Elstir, 'vous avez été déçu par ce porche, mais c'est la plus belle Bible historiée que le peuple ait jamais pu lire' (II, p.196), and then proceeds to give the Narrator a lengthy and detailed lesson in medieval iconography, ending with the down-to-earth assertion that 'Le type qui a sculpté cette façade-là, croyez bien qu'il était aussi fort, qu'il avait des idées aussi profondes que les gens de maintenant que vous admirez le plus' (II, p.197; note the expression of depth once again). Elstir's lecture is a corrective to the Narrator's over-emotional approach to art: it is all very well having your heart in the right place, but you must exercise your intellect at the same time, keeping a balance between the two. This is, for once, advice which the Narrator heeds.

Vinteuil

Much more could be said about Bergotte and Elstir, but greatest attention needs to be paid to Vinteuil: his artistic example is the clinching one. At first, such an eventuality seems highly unlikely: at Combray (again, there is a firm identification with place), Vinteuil is an excessively modest person, the archetypal piano-teacher (see I, pp.110-11). So retiring is he, in fact, that when Swann encounters the *Violin Sonata* by a certain Vinteuil, he assumes it to be by a different person (I, pp.210-11). It is a classic case of appearances being misleading, a recurrent theme in Proust. As for the music itself, it is well known that a 'petite phrase' from the sonata is artificially dislodged and used by Swann to perform the function of 'national anthem' of his and Odette's love (I, p.215), but Swann's appreciation of the music is not quite as philistine as this might lead one to believe: the presentation by the third-person narrator makes this clear:

> Peut-être est-ce parce qu'il [Swann] ne savait pas la musique qu'il avait pu éprouver une impression aussi confuse, une de ces impressions qui sont peut-être pourtant les seules purement musicales, inétendues, entièrement originales, irréductibles à tout autre ordre d'impressions. Une impression de ce genre, pendant un instant, est pour ainsi dire *sine materia*. (I, p.206)

What we have here is simultaneously a tribute to the power of music (even to an untrained ear) and the beginnings of a theory of what constitutes that power: the emotional effect and the intellectual explanation. For the Narrator, if not for Swann, this recognition of the transcendental nature of music always goes hand-in-hand with a desire to comprehend the phenomenon in as rational a manner as possible. Whenever the Narrator (here very close to Proust himself) expatiates about music, he does so with exemplary knowledge and authority.

But music is not some lofty, unattainable concept: it is an everyday experience, available to all, moving in both senses of the word:

> Quand ce qui est le plus caché dans la Sonate de Vinteuil se découvrit à moi, déjà, entraîné par l'habitude hors des prises de ma sensibilité, ce que j'avais distingué, préféré tout d'abord, commençait à m'échapper, à me fuir. Pour n'avoir pu aimer qu'en des temps successifs tout ce que m'apportait cette Sonate, je ne la possédai jamais tout entière: elle ressemblait à la vie.
>
> (I, p.521)

The Narrator cannot know it at the time, but this recognition of the fugitive nature of things will characterise his relationship with Albertine. For him art and life are indeed inextricably linked, but he never makes Swann's blunder and debases art: art will not abide being trivialised. And while Swann is content to associate the 'petite phrase' with a single emotional configuration, the Narrator characteristically moves on to a higher plane, associating it with 'notre condition mortelle' and 'la réalité de notre âme', whilst engaging in metaphysical speculation about the effect of music in general:

> Peut-être est-ce le néant qui est le vrai et tout notre rêve est-il inexistant, mais alors nous sentons qu'il faudra que ces phrases musicales, ces notions qui existent par rapport à lui, ne soient rien non plus. Nous périrons, mais nous avons pour otages ces captives divines qui suivront notre chance. Et la mort avec elles a quelque chose de moins amer, de moins inglorieux, peut-être de moins probable. (I, pp.344-45)

The content and structure of this last sentence inescapably recall sentences employed by the Narrator in the midst of the madeleine episode: 'Il [un plaisir délicieux] m'avait aussitôt rendu les vicissitudes de la vie indifférentes, ses désastres inoffensifs, sa brièveté illusoire. [...] J'avais cessé de me sentir médiocre, contingent, mortel' (I, p.44). The forceful tripartite ordering allied to metaphysical vocabulary applied to the individual emphatically designates the attainment of a state above that of ordinary experience – a state of exaltation. This common denominator between a *moment bienheureux* and an artistically-engendered condition of euphoria will be fully explored and explained later in the novel – much later, in fact, because there is a considerable dearth of musical experience, and of Vinteuil's music in particular, in the central, socially-oriented parts of *A la recherche du temps perdu*. While not totally a cultural desert for the Narrator (we have seen him admiring the duc de Guermantes's collection of Elstirs), this period is one where art is subordinated to the demands of society and of the affair with Albertine. When the revelation comes, it is absolute.

The event in question is the first performance of Vinteuil's posthumous *Septet*, at a Verdurin reception (III, pp.753-70); it is widely regarded as the most brilliant evocation of music in literature (see *47*). But the event has its darker side: it takes place at the height of Albertine's imprisonment, when life is most claustrophobic for the Narrator; and, irony of ironies, the performance of the work has been made possible only by the efforts of the infamous 'amie de Mlle Vinteuil', who performed the seemingly impossible task of deciphering the musician's chaotic manuscript. All of this augurs badly for the Narrator. Yet he is shaken out of his gloomy state of mind as soon as the music starts: he recognises the sonata's 'petite phrase' – an unexpected encounter like those in the *Arabian Nights* – now 'harnachée d'argent, toute ruisselante de sonorités brillantes, légères et douces'; the composer has opened up for the listener 'un univers inconnu', but one which is strangely familiar, in the shape of the Combray church-bells; Vinteuil is 'réincarné', he 'vivait à jamais dans sa musique'; each of

his works is 'une même prière, jaillie devant différents levers de
soleil intérieurs'; they represent '[d']éternelles investigations' of
which we can 'mesurer la profondeur' (depth again), but which we
cannot translate into human language; each true artist is in this way
'le citoyen d'une patrie inconnue, oubliée de lui-même, différente de
celle d'où viendra, appareillant pour la terre, un autre grand artiste'
(III, pp.753-61, *passim*). Shot through with metaphysical vocabulary
and spiritual fervour, the passage culminates in an astonishing
heaven-storming peroration:

> Des ailes, un autre appareil respiratoire, et qui nous
> permissent de traverser l'immensité, ne nous serviraient
> à rien. Car si nous allions dans Mars et dans Vénus en
> gardant les mêmes sens, ils revêtiraient du même aspect
> que les choses de la Terre tout ce que nous pourrions
> voir. Le seul véritable voyage, le seul bain de Jouvence,
> ce ne serait pas d'aller vers de nouveaux paysages, mais
> d'avoir d'autres yeux, de voir l'univers avec les yeux
> d'un autre, de cent autres, de voir les cent univers que
> chacun d'eux voit, que chacun d'eux est: et cela nous le
> pouvons avec un Elstir, avec un Vinteuil, avec leurs
> pareils, nous volons vraiment d'étoiles en étoiles.
>
> (III, p.762)

Nor is this all: the 'joie ineffable qui semblait venir du
paradis', this 'révélation' ties in precisely with

> ces impressions qu'à des intervalles éloignés je
> retrouvais dans ma vie comme les points de repère, les
> amorces pour la construction d'une vie véritable:
> l'impression éprouvée devant les clochers de Martin-
> ville, devant une rangée d'arbres près de Balbec.
>
> (III, p.765),

in other words, with the *moments bienheureux*. In making this
linkage, the Narrator explicitly creates a point of intersection

between his persona as protagonist and his persona as potential creator: up to now, he has been a passive observer and has mostly just let things happen to him; now, with the fillip of the Vinteuil *Septet*, he is impelled to the active recognition that his own personal metaphysical experiences are intimately connected to the essence of art. The 'construction d'une vie véritable' can begin, but this time it is life which has learned the lesson of art.

In a crucial passage close to the end of *La Prisonnière*, the Narrator repeats the comparison of Vinteuil's music to the *moments bienheureux*, adding, 'plus simplement', the madeleine episode (III, p.877). It is crucial because what follows is a conversation about art with Albertine, whose 'love' will be superseded precisely by art, just as she is shortly to disappear from the scene. In a magisterial survey of how to identify the fingerprints of greatness in musicians and writers, the Narrator performs exactly the same role as Elstir had in explaining the marvels of Balbec church. One senses at last – and here is firm evidence for it – that he has served his apprenticeship to art and is capable not only of speaking with discernment about it, but actually creating it himself.

The Narrator

'Qu'était-ce autre chose que faire une œuvre d'art?' This final realisation is a supremely logical one, for the Narrator is permitted, through hindsight, to discern a pattern in his life which inescapably points to an artistic fulfilment. The work of art is 'le seul moyen de retrouver le Temps perdu' (IV, p.478); further, 'je compris que tous ces matériaux de l'œuvre littéraire, c'était ma vie passée' (ibid.). So the major justification and raw materials of the enterprise are clear enough, but what about the detail? And most specifically, what about the manner of the writing, its theoretical basis?

Substantial portions of *Le Temps retrouvé* are given over to considerations of literary theory, pages which some critics have found dry and unnovelistic. An exacerbating feature is deemed to be the clearly unpolished state of the text at this point. I prefer to view these 'defects' in a more positive fashion. For a start, the Narrator, before embarking on his work, must surely engage with critical theory if he is to exercise the intellectual rigour proper to such an ambitious venture: these concerns cannot be taken for granted. Then, the staccato review of different literary techniques, even if it does appear rough, seems appropriate to a person in a hurry, discarding each theory as rapidly as it is evoked, in a sequence of theoretical 'bites'. Finally, it must be remembered that the future work of art is now actually the plot of the novel we are reading and is susceptible to the same sort of treatment in depth as, say, a major character. There is a developing story-line to these parts of *Le Temps retrouvé* which possesses its own brand of drama.

The basic programme which the Narrator adopts is one of discovery:

> Ainsi j'étais déjà arrivé à cette conclusion que nous
> ne sommes nullement libres devant l'œuvre d'art, que
> nous ne la faisons pas à notre gré, mais que, préexistant
> à nous, nous devons, à la fois parce qu'elle est néces-
> saire et cachée, et comme nous ferions pour une loi de la
> nature, la découvrir. (IV, p.459)

The pattern of disclosing what lies under the surface is a familiar one; what becomes crucial now is the methodology employed, for there are many ways of expressing such disclosure in literature. Theory must be applied, but it is a means to an end, not an end in itself: 'Une œuvre où il y a des théories est comme un objet sur lequel on laisse la marque du prix' (IV, p.461). So-called realism, the sort of literature which 'se contente de "décrire les choses"' and which only gives 'un misérable relevé de lignes et de surfaces' is a sad thing, because it 'coupe brusquement toute communication de notre moi présent avec le passé' (IV, pp.463-64). As for popular and patriotic art, the concepts strike the Narrator as being ridiculous, if not dangerous:

> A cet égard, un art populaire par la forme eût été destiné
> plutôt aux membres du Jockey qu'à ceux de la

> Confédération générale du travail; quant aux sujets, les
> romans populaires ennuient autant les gens du peuple
> que les enfants ces livres qui sont écrits pour eux. On
> cherche à se dépayser en lisant, et les ouvriers sont aussi
> curieux des princes que les princes des ouvriers.
> (IV, p.467)

The Narrator is pragmatic in his judgements, preferring common
sense over dogmatism. Once again, as so often, he appeals to the
deeper aspects of human experience, in condemning another literary
tendency:

> Comment la littérature de notations aurait-elle une
> valeur quelconque, puisque c'est sous de petites choses
> comme celles qu'elle note que la réalité est contenue (la
> grandeur dans le bruit lointain d'un aéroplane, dans la
> ligne du clocher de Saint-Hilaire, le passé dans la saveur
> d'une madeleine, etc.) et qu'elles sont sans signification
> par elles-mêmes si on ne l'en dégage pas? (IV, p.473)

Up to this point, the Narrator has been largely negative in his
assessments of various theoretical camps; but he had begun his
survey with a positive assertion – the one about discovery – and he
returns to it in the last words of this passage, in a suitably forward-
looking rhetorical question.

There is now no looking back: 'La vraie vie, la vie enfin
découverte et éclaircie, la seule vie par conséquent pleinement
vécue, c'est la littérature' (IV, p.474). A new voice of self-
confidence rings forth, the Narrator now certain he has chosen the
right path: 'ce qu'il s'agit de faire sortir, d'amener à la lumière, ce
sont nos sentiments, nos passions, c'est-à-dire les passions, les
sentiments de tous' (IV, p.486). Literature alone permits this
opening-out to others, this to-and-fro between what is particular and
what is general, so that, in a famous phrase, 'en réalité, chaque
lecteur est quand il lit le propre lecteur de soi-même' (IV, p.489).
Literature is like an optical instrument which permits the reader to

'discerner ce que sans ce livre il n'eût peut-être pas vu en soi-même' (IV, p.490).

On the specific material of his experience – and hence of the work-to-be – the Narrator pays signal tribute to Swann: it was he who, in Combray, inspired him to go to Balbec, thus initiating a sequence of events and acquaintances which he could never have foreseen. Even the welter of *moments bienheureux* which he has just experienced in the courtyard and house of the prince de Guermantes are in a sense attributable to Swann, so that he owes him 'non seulement la matière mais, la décision' regarding the book (IV, p.494). Thus a single individual clearly makes the point about the importance of what appears at first trivial – who could have believed what ramifications would issue from a few social visits paid by a certain 'M. Swann' in a Combray garden? A realisation such as this brings with it a guarantee of authenticity, a sort of self-validating authority (IV, p.457), just as the random nature of the *moments bienheureux* does.

But the process of discovery is not a straightforward one of simply tracing backwards in time: it entails a veritable effort of translation. For it is a matter of interpreting signs, working out what these 'caractères hiéroglyphiques' represent (IV, p.457):

> Je m'apercevais que ce livre essentiel, le seul livre vrai,
> un grand écrivain n'a pas, dans le sens courant, à
> l'inventer puisqu'il existe déjà en chacun de nous, mais
> à le traduire. Le devoir et la tâche d'un écrivain sont
> ceux d'un traducteur. (IV, p.469)

This notion directly links up with remarks made at the crucial Vinteuil *Septet* concert. Vinteuil who 'chant[ait] selon sa patrie' (III, p.761), and whose hieroglyphs his daughter's infamous friend deciphered for posterity's benefit (III, p.765). And the great musician's name is finally invoked in the context of the Guermantes reception set of *moments bienheureux*, when the Narrator groups these events with earlier sensations such as the madeleine, and asserts that 'les dernières œuvres de Vinteuil m'avaient paru [les]

synthétiser' (IV, p.445). Last of all, beyond this internal aesthetic
validation, the Narrator seeks endorsement in the shape of
illustrious literary antecedents: the examples of Chateaubriand,
Nerval and Baudelaire – all of whom show *moments bienheureux* at
work – leave him in no doubt that 'l'œuvre que je n'avais plus
aucune hésitation à entreprendre méritait l'effort que j'allais lui
consacrer' (IV, p.499).

Even the rude interruption in the Narrator's meditations
represented by his being admitted to the reception fails to daunt
him. One hundred pages attest to the adverse work of time on
friends re-met after many years, and would be discouraging in
normal circumstances, but it is not so. And when Gilberte presents
her and Robert de Saint-Loup's daughter to him, uniting as she does
the Swann and Guermantes 'côtés', it seems as if everything has
turned full circle:

> Je la trouvais bien belle: pleine encore d'espérances,
> riante, formée des années mêmes que j'avais perdues,
> elle ressemblait à ma jeunesse. (IV, p.609)

So by the simplest – and most touching – of transitions, the Narrator
returns to his main theme and proceeds to his very final
meditations. Drawing all manner of parallels with the work he is
about to embark upon, he likens its preparations to a military
offensive, to building a church, to following a diet. Françoise helps
him at the physical work of putting his manuscript into shape:
'épinglant ici un feuillet supplémentaire, je bâtirais mon livre, je
n'ose pas dire ambitieusement comme une cathédrale, mais tout
simplement comme une robe' (IV, p.610). For a person who sets his
artistic sights so high, the Narrator retains a moving humility.

Even at the point of greatest assertion, a characteristic note of
doubt is sounded:

> L'idée de ma construction ne me quittait pas un instant.
> Je ne savais pas si ce serait une église où des fidèles
> sauraient peu à peu apprendre des vérités et découvrir

des harmonies, le grand plan d'ensemble, ou si cela
resterait – comme un monument druidique au sommet
d'une île – quelque chose d'infréquenté à jamais.

(IV, pp.617-18)

In truth, there is no real doubt here: even the negative possibility is
conceived of in artistic terms (the 'monument druidique'). As for
the positive component advanced, it brings together in the pithiest
manner two major artistic preoccupations of the Narrator –
architecture and music. With more and more frequent references to
Combray as the novel nears its conclusion, the mention here of a
church inevitably recalls the ringing eulogy of Combray church in
the first volume, together with its reverberations on to Balbec
church and the artistic complex represented by Elstir. Then, this
church which is the fiction-to-be contains music expressive of truths
– the Vinteuil *Septet* springs straight to mind. Finally, the religious
aura which the Narrator summons up at this point could not more
eloquently recapitulate what has underpinned his artistic *credo* all
along: faith in the power of art to transcend and give meaning to
life. 'La vraie vie, la vie enfin découverte et éclaircie' (IV, p.474).

7. Proust as Classic

It has become clear that for a good many readers Proust is now not just the greatest French novelist of the twentieth century, but the greatest of all French novelists. (23, p.xiii)

On a longtemps dit que, si l'Angleterre possédait Shakespeare, l'Allemagne Goethe, l'Italie Dante, la France n'avait personne qui les égalât. Le nombre des travaux qui lui sont consacrés donne à penser qu'elle a maintenant, qu'elle aura demain Marcel Proust.

(I, pp.x-xi)

Why is Proust so important? How is it that critics can arrive at such a lofty assessment of his novel? His eminence emerges very clearly from even the briefest perusal of the manner in which he has been critically received over the past eighty years or so. If some of the first reactions to *Du côté de chez Swann* registered bewilderment ('It's impossible to make head or tail of it!' exclaimed a publisher's reader in 1912: see *33*, p.75), others displayed more comprehension, and were positive in their response. A very early review, by Mary Duclaux in the *Times Literary Supplement* of 4 December 1913, speaks of 'the fresh and fine reality which these pages mysteriously recover from the back of our consciousness. [...] Something older and deeper than knowledge pervades the book' (*33*, p.91), recognition along lines which will become familiar.

After the delay occasioned by the Great War, the story of the novel's critical reception has been one of unmitigated success: Proust is rare amongst writers in never having known a period of eclipse. The *Hommage* which the *Nouvelle Revue Française* published in Proust's memory in 1923 was in many ways an act of consecration which set the tone for much subsequent criticism. An important aspect of the *Hommage* was its international flavour, with contributions from eminent non-French critics, notably a group of English writers, and the great German Romance scholar Ernst Robert Curtius. Almost from the beginning, the response to Proust is a cosmopolitan one, and things have stayed that way ever since, attracting minds of the highest calibre. In recent decades, all manner of critical theories have been brought to bear on Proust, with varying degrees of success, it is true, but always in implicit recognition that he represents the ultimate test of any given theory. So we have had existentialist, structuralist, deconstructionist and reader-response approaches. The list will certainly not end there.

But all this criticism is really only second-hand approbation. The fact is, Proust has entered the common consciousness sufficiently for sympathetic readers to become, quite naturally, what Proust's Narrator would like them to be, 'les propres lecteurs d'eux-mêmes' (IV, p.610). Concepts such as this – and, generally speaking, what might be termed a 'Proustian sensibility' – have become such common currency that one no longer registers surprise at what must once have seemed new and daring. It is now almost normal that a work of art should contain within itself its own set of interpretative guidelines: in *A la recherche du temps perdu*, these guidelines constitute a programme of action for the Narrator; for the reader, a set of eminently sensible suggestions. Why had no one thought of this before?

Generally speaking, there is a feeling of great sense in all that Proust's Narrator advocates in these final pages of the novel. When, for example, he opts for an artistic life, he could not be further from prescribing an ivory-tower existence:

> Dès le début de la guerre M. Barrès avait dit que l'artiste [...] doit avant tout servir la gloire de sa patrie. Mais il ne peut la servir qu'en étant artiste, c'est-à-dire qu'à condition, au moment où il étudie ces lois, institue

> ces expériences et fait ces découvertes, aussi délicates
> que celles de la science, de ne pas penser à autre chose –
> fût-e à la patrie – qu'à la vérité qui est devant lui.
>
> (IV, p.467)

It takes considerable courage to adopt a principled stand in
jingoistic times, and against an eminent author who stopped writing
novels in order to chronicle the war. But what is more read, more
valued today: Barrès's *Chronique de la Grande Guerre*, or the
wartime pages of *A la recherche du temps perdu*?

Similarly, the artistic justifications articulated in *Le Temps
retrouvé* are often illustrated by Proust in such a way as to arouse in
the reader common, if hazily perceived, feelings. The sight of
George Sand's *François le Champi* in the Guermantes' library, for
instance, gives rise to meditations on the notion of what constitutes
a 'first edition':

> La première édition d'un ouvrage m'eût été plus
> précieuse que les autres, mais j'aurais entendu par elle
> l'édition où je le lus pour la première fois. Je
> rechercherais les éditions originales, je veux dire celles
> où j'eus de ce livre une impression originale. Car les
> impressions suivantes ne le sont plus. Je collectionnerais
> pour les romans les reliures d'autrefois, celles du temps
> où je lus mes premiers romans et qui entendaient tant de
> fois papa me dire: 'Tiens-toi droit!' (IV, p.465)

The homely touch of the last sentence gives just the right degree of
intimacy to enable the reader to make an effortless transition to his
or her own experience: what might otherwise have remained in the
realms of dry abstraction is, by its very precision of example, made
generally available and congenial.

This shifting perspective on commonly-held notions runs right
through *A la recherche du temps perdu*. Earlier on, the Narrator
had tackled the concept of 'first hearing', in connection with his
experience of Vinteuil's *Sonata*:

> Si l'on n'avait vraiment, comme on l'a cru, rien
> distingué à la première audition, la deuxième, la
> troisième, seraient autant de premières, et il n'y aurait
> pas de raison pour qu'on comprît quelque chose de plus
> à la dixième. (I, p.520)

Personal experience serves to modify strict logic along more
amenable lines, consonant with the fallibility of human perceptions.
There is a rhythm of loss and gain here which is familiar to all:

> Moins décevants que la vie, ces grands chefs-d'œuvre
> ne commencent pas par nous donner ce qu'ils ont de
> meilleur. Dans la Sonate de Vinteuil les beautés qu'on
> découvre le plus tôt sont aussi celles dont on se fatigue
> le plus vite et pour la même raison sans doute, qui est
> qu'elles diffèrent moins de ce qu'on connaissait déjà.
> Mais quand celles-là se sont éloignées, il nous reste à
> aimer telle phrase que son ordre trop nouveau pour
> offrir à notre esprit rien que confusion nous avait rendue
> indiscernable et gardée intacte; alors elle devant qui
> nous passions tous les jours sans le savoir et qui s'était
> réservée, qui par le pouvoir de sa seule beauté était
> devenue invisible et restée inconnue, elle vient à nous la
> dernière. Mais nous la quitterons aussi en dernier.

> (I, p.521)

Proust succeeds in rendering a personal experience (doubly
personal, because the object of study is itself fictional) immediately
accessible to the reader by a no-nonsense evocation of the passage of
time and of how it is perceptible in everyday life. Similarly, the
presentation of Mlle de Saint-Loup (quoted in the previous chapter:
'elle ressemblait à ma jeunesse') is brought off with brilliant
immediacy. The very economy of means enables volumes to be
spoken – a few deft strokes of evocation, no more, and the reader
readily slips into those first-person pronouns used by the Narrator.

This is a far cry from the 'signification philosophique infinie' with which the youthful Narrator had sought to infuse his yet-to-be-written masterpieces (I, p.170), and all the better for being so. In stressing that personal experience is paramount, Proust is supremely the poet of the ordinary, but 'ordinary' only in the sense that a great author can dare to be. What lesser author, having produced a *magnum opus*, would have the self-effacement to claim that it 'n'éta[i]t qu'une sorte de ces verres grossissants comme ceux que tendait à un acheteur l'opticien de Combray' (IV, p.610)? This is the sort of audacious simplicity which Shakespeare, Dante and Goethe display in abundance, and which enables them effortlessly to bridge the gap between the particular and the general. Or rather, with them as with Proust, there is effectively no gap: here is no imposition of privileged experience, but a sharing of common experience. In speaking of himself, the writer speaks with and for everyone: in an inspired phrase of Proust's, it is 'un égoïsme utilisable pour autrui' (IV, p.613).

For all the indubitable excellences in Proust's work, this pervading sense of modesty is perhaps what lingers most after a reading of the novel. The acute insights and verbal felicities of which the Narrator is capable are made to seem easily performable by ourselves, because we are made of the same fallible stuff as he. This surely is Proust's greatest contribution to literature, that he manages to make each reader identify so closely with his Narrator as to seem to participate in the creative act itself. It was well put in the *Hommage* of 1923 by a group of English writers (including Joseph Conrad and Virginia Woolf, no less):

> Nous sentions qu'apparaissait un nouveau grand écrivain français, qui nous offrait une peinture magnifique et neuve de cette vie de Paris et de la province française sur laquelle notre curiosité ne sera jamais rassasiée. Mais notre impression allait plus loin encore: dans la *Recherche du temps perdu* Marcel Proust nous semblait avoir retrouvé non seulement son propre passé, mais aussi le nôtre, au point de nous

> restituer à nous-mêmes et de nous rendre la vie telle que
> nous l'avions connue et sentie – notre expérience banale
> de chaque jour – mais enrichie, embellie, magnifiée par
> l'alchimie de l'art. (*34*, pp.248-49)

These words are as true today as when they were written so long ago. The tale of *A la recherche du temps perdu* is not just that of some seemingly inconsequential human beings in turn-of-the-century France, it is the tale of us all. And while we may stand in awe of Proust's achievement, we feel that, yes, we too hold within ourselves equivalent grandeur.

Appendix

An Outline of 'A la recherche du temps perdu'

In *Du côté de chez Swann*, we witness the Narrator's recall of his childhood in Combray, and later on in Paris. An interpolation deals with Swann's affair with Odette. *A l'ombre des jeunes filles en fleurs* continues the Narrator's growing-up in Paris (notably with Gilberte Swann), and on holiday at Balbec, where he meets Robert de Saint-Loup, M. de Charlus, and Albertine Simonet. In *Le Côté de Guermantes*, the Narrator's family have moved to a wing of that aristocratic family's Paris house, and he is greatly preoccupied with the social scene; his grandmother dies in harrowing circumstances. Much of *Sodome et Gomorrhe* is given over to investigation of the substrata of society, notably homosexuality: M. de Charlus is an exemplary figure here. A second visit to Balbec succeeds in cementing the Narrator's involvement with Albertine, the jealousy and suspicion of which are chronicled in *La Prisonnière*, back in Paris. The title of *Albertine disparue* hides a double disappearance: first she flees, then is killed in a riding accident. The Narrator must submit to the slow process of forgetting: a trip to Venice helps. But he is close to breakdown and, as war erupts, seeks treatment in various sanatoria. Returning to Paris (at the beginning of *Le Temps retrouvé*), he finds all is changed, everyone has grown grotesquely older, and the social scene has been turned on its head. Nevertheless, a sequence of metaphysical experiences convinces the Narrator that he must waste no further time, and fulfil his literary vocation, latent from the outset. He will take as subject-matter his own past life, and transform it into art.

Select Bibliography

The number of books and articles devoted to Proust is now so vast that only a limited selection can be presented.

PROUST'S WORKS

1. *A la recherche du temps perdu*, edited by J.-Y. Tadié (4 vols, Paris, Gallimard, Bibliothèque de la Pléiade, 1987-89). This near-definitive edition (which contains a brilliant introduction and large amounts of preliminary sketches) is likely to remain the standard text for many years to come. Reliable and well-documented paperback editions are available in the Bouquins, Folio, Garnier-Flammarion and Livre de poche series.
2. *Jean Santeuil, précédé de Les Plaisirs et les jours* (Paris, Gallimard, Bibliothèque de la Pléiade, 1971).
3. *Contre Sainte-Beuve, précédé de Pastiches et Mélanges et suivi de Essais et articles* (Paris, Gallimard, Bibliothèque de la Pléiade, 1971).
4. *Ecrits de jeunesse* (Paris, Institut Marcel Proust International, 1991).
5. *Textes retrouvés*, edited by Philip Kolb (Paris, Gallimard, 1971).
6. *Le Carnet de 1908*, edited by Philip Kolb (Paris, Gallimard, 1976).

   (Items 2-6 all contain important early texts by Proust.)

7. *Matinée chez la princesse de Guermantes*, edited by Henry Bonnet and Bernard Brun (Paris, Gallimard, 1982).
8. *Bricquebec*, edited by Richard Bales (Oxford, Oxford University Press, 1989).
9. Alden, D. *Marcel Proust's Grasset Proofs* (Chapel Hill, University of North Carolina Press, 1978).

   (Items 7-9 contain extended early versions of important episodes in *A la recherche du temps perdu*.)

10. *Correspondance de Marcel Proust*, edited by Philip Kolb (21 vols, Paris, Plon, 1970-93). A monument of twentieth-century scholarship, the late Philip Kolb's magisterial edition reveals Proust as one of the great letter-writers. Invaluable background to the works.

BIOGRAPHY

11. Diesbach, G. de. *Proust* (Paris, Perrin, 1991). The most recent biography, and a reliable one.

12. Maurois, A. *A la recherche de Marcel Proust* (Paris, Hachette, 1949). Still well worth reading.

13. Painter, G.D. *Marcel Proust* (2 vols, London, Chatto & Windus, 1959, 1965; often reprinted). Criticised on its appearance for some liberties taken with the relationship between Proust's life and his works, it nevertheless rapidly became, and has remained, the standard biography.

BIBLIOGRAPHY

14. Graham, V.E. *Bibliographie des études sur Marcel Proust* (Geneva, Droz, 1976).

15. Rancœur, R. 'Bibliographie de Marcel Proust', in *Etudes proustiennes* (Paris, Gallimard, 1973, 1975, 1979, 1982, 1984, 1987).

CRITICAL WORKS

16. Alden, D.W. *Marcel Proust and his French Critics* (New York, Russell and Russell, 1940; reprinted 1973).

17. Bales, R. *Proust and the Middle Ages* (Geneva, Droz, 1975).

18. Bardèche, M. *Marcel Proust romancier* (2 vols, Paris, Les Sept Couleurs, 1971).

19. Bonnet, H. *Marcel Proust de 1907 à 1914* (2 vols, Paris, Nizet, 1971, 1976). Indispensable for the genesis of Proust's novel.

20. Bowie, M. *Freud, Proust and Lacan* (Cambridge, Cambridge University Press, 1987). Psychological theory and imaginative literature.

21. Bucknall, B. *The Religion of Art in Proust* (Urbana, University of Illinois Press, 1969).

22. Butor, M. *Les Œuvres d'art imaginaires chez Proust* (London, Athlone Press, 1964); included in *Essais sur les modernes* (Paris, Gallimard, 1964), pp.129-97. Some of the most penetrating writing on the topic.

23. Cocking, J.M. *Proust: Collected Essays on the Writer and his Art* (Cambridge, Cambridge University Press, 1982). Exceptionally profound criticism.

24. Collier, P. *Proust and Venice* (Cambridge, Cambridge University Press, 1989).
25. Compagnon, A. *Proust entre deux siècles* (Paris, Seuil, 1989).
26. Deleuze, G. *Marcel Proust et les signes* (Paris, P.U.F., 1964; second edition 1970). Challenging semiotic study.
27. Ellison, R. *The Reading of Proust* (Oxford, Basil Blackwell, 1984). The importance of reading for Proust himself and within his novel.
28. Ferré, A. *Géographie de Marcel Proust* (Paris, Editions du Sagittaire, 1939). Remains an essential book.
29. Fraisse, L. *Le Processus de la création chez Marcel Proust: le fragment expérimental* (Paris, Corti, 1988). A very important book on Proust's compositional methods.
30. Genette, G. *Figures III* (Paris, Seuil, 1972). An impressive structuralist approach.
31. Graham, V.E. *The Imagery of Proust* (Oxford, Basil Blackwell, 1966).
32. Hindus, M. *The Proustian Vision* (New York, Columbia University Press, 1954).
33. Hodson, L. *Marcel Proust: the Critical Heritage* (London, Routledge, 1989). An invaluable anthology of the early reception of Proust's works up to 1931.
34. *Hommage à Marcel Proust* (Paris, N.R.F., 1923; reprinted 1990). The memorial tribute.
35. Hughes, E.J. *Marcel Proust: A Study in the Quality of Awareness* (Cambridge, Cambridge University Press, 1983).
36. Kasell, W. *Marcel Proust and the Strategy of Reading* (Amsterdam, John Benjamins, 1980).
37. Kilmartin, T. *A Guide to Proust* (London, Chatto & Windus, 1983; reprinted Harmondsworth, Penguin, 1985). A helpful little encyclopedia.
38. Milly, J. *La Phrase de Proust* (Paris, Larousse, 1975; reprinted Geneva, Slatkine, 1983).
39. ——. *Proust et le style* (Paris, Minard, 1970).
40. Muller, M. *Les Voix narratives dans la 'Recherche du temps perdu'* (Geneva, Droz, 1965; reprinted 1983).
41. Nattiez, J.-J. *Proust musicien* (Paris, Christian Bourgois, 1984).
42. Newman-Gordon, P. *Dictionnaire des idées dans l'œuvre de Marcel Proust* (The Hague and Paris, Mouton, 1968).
43. ——. *Proust et l'existentialisme* (Paris, Nouvelles Editions Latines, 1952).
44. Pugh, A.R. *The Birth of 'A la recherche du temps perdu'* (Lexington, Kentucky, French Forum, 1987). A close-up study of a crucial year in the life of Proust's novel.

45. Richard, J.-P. *Proust et le monde sensible* (Paris, Seuil, 1974).
     Allusive and penetrating.
46. Rogers, B.G. *Proust's Narrative Techniques* (Geneva, Droz, 1965).
47. Said, E. *Musical Elaborations* (London, Chatto & Windus, 1991).
     Places Proust on music in a wider musical context.
48. Shattuck, R. *Proust* (London, Fontana, 1974). A marvellous little
     book: contains some of the best Proust criticism ever written.
49. ——. *Proust's Binoculars* (London, Chatto & Windus, 1964). Equally
     desirable.
50. Slater, M. *Humour in the Works of Proust* (Oxford, Oxford University
     Press, 1979).
51. Strauss, W.A. *Proust and Literature* (Cambridge, Mass., Harvard
     University Press, 1957).
52. Tadié, J.-Y. *Proust et le roman* (Paris, Gallimard, 1971; reprinted
     1986). An essential study.
53. ——. *Proust* (Paris, Belfond, 1983). A magisterial survey of main
     themes and associated criticism.
54. Winton, A. *Proust's Additions* (Cambridge, Cambridge University
     Press, 1977). Details the additions Proust made to his novel during the
     First World War.

There are three periodicals devoted to Proust: the *Bulletin de la Société des Amis de Marcel Proust et des Amis de Combray* (28120 Illiers-Combray); the *Bulletin d'Informations Proustiennes* (Ecole Normale Supérieure, Paris); and the *Proust Research Association Newsletter* (University of Kansas).

CRITICAL GUIDES TO FRENCH TEXTS

edited by
Roger Little, Wolfgang van Emden, David Williams